RESCUE

God and Sin in the Old Testament

JOHN F. WAKEFIELD

CYPRESS
PUBLICATIONS
An Imprint of Heritage Christian University Press

Copyright © 2021 by John F. Wakefield

Cataloging-in-Publication Data

Wakefield, John F.

Rescue: God and sin the Old Testament / by John F. Wakefield

p. cm.

Includes bibliographic references (p.) and indexes.

ISBN 978-1-0879-5552-0(pbk.) 978-1-0879-5553-7 (ebook)

1. Bible. Old Testament—Criticism, interpretation, etc. I. Author. II. Title.

221.6—DC20

Library of Congress Control Number: 20221905867

Cover design by Brad McKinnon and Brittany Vander Maas

Interior design by Brad McKinnon

All rights reserved.

No part of this book may be reproduced in any form or by any electronic or mechanical means, including information storage and retrieval systems, without written permission from the author, except for the use of brief quotations in a book review.

"Only a Holy God" Copyright © 2016 CityAlight Music (APRA) Farren Love And War Pub (SESAC) Integrity's Alleluia! Music (SESAC) Integrity's Praise! Music (BMI) (adm. at CapitolCMGPublishing.com) All rights reserved. Used by permission.

Scripture quotations marked NASB taken from the New American Standard Bible® (NASB), Copyright © 1960, 1962, 1963, 1968, 1971, 1972, 1973, 1975, 1977, 1995 by The Lockman Foundation. Used by permission. www.Lockman.org

For Janelle

CONTENTS

Foreword	ix
Prologue	1
Abbreviations	3
Preface	7
1. What Is a Spiritual Rescue?	11
2. Rescue from an Evil World	27
3. Rescue from Self-Righteousness	43
4. Rescue from Doubt	59
5. Failed Rescue from Unintentional Sin	78
6. Rescue from Covetousness	93
7. Rescue from Idolatry Refused	109
8. Rescue from a Sinful Past	125
9. Rescue from Multiple Sins	142
10. Rescue from Fear	161
11. Rescue from Willful Sin	179
12. Conclusions	195
Appendix	209
Notes	217
Bibliography	221
Scripture Index	225
About the Author	233
Also by Cypress Publications	235

RESCUE

FOREWORD

With the publication of *Rescue: God and Sin in the Old Testament*, Dr. John Wakefield has provided a useful resource for all who have a working knowledge of Old Testament stories but who want to think more deeply about spiritual rescues carried out by God in the Old Testament. Dr. Wakefield's career in higher education and his years of experience as a shepherd in the Lord's church have served him well in crafting a book that is interesting, thought-provoking, and easy to read.

Rescue is unique in that Wakefield employs an informal case study approach to exploring the spiritual rescues he has included in the book. These case studies are assembled by drawing from multiple data sources within the Bible thereby providing a broad perspective on the events included. While the names associated with these case studies are familiar (Noah, Job, Abraham, Sarah, Hagar, Lot, Jacob, Rahab, David, Elijah, and Jonah), thinking in terms of a spiritual rescue is sure to result in a better understanding of these people whose names we have known since we first became students of the Bible.

With the inclusion of study questions at the end of each chapter, *Rescue: God and Sin in the Old Testament* is well-suited for both individual and group study, such as a Bible class. I am blessed to count Dr. John Wakefield as both a friend and a brother, and I am confident you will enjoy *Rescue*!

Philip Goad, Minister
    North Highlands Church of Christ, Russellville, Alabama

PROLOGUE

Who else could rescue me from my failing?
Who else would offer His only Son?
Who else invites me to call Him Father?
Only a Holy God,
Only my Holy God!"

-Lyrics from *Only a Holy God* by CityAlight

ABBREVIATIONS

Old Testament
Gen	Genesis
Exod	Exodus
Lev	Leviticus
Num	Numbers
Deut	Deuteronomy
Josh	Joshua
Judg	Judges
Ruth	Ruth
1–2 Sam	1–2 Samuel
1–2 Kgs	1–2 Kings
1–2 Chr	1–2 Chronicles
Ezra	Ezra
Neh	Nehemiah
Esth	Esther
Job	Job
Ps	Psalms
Prov	Proverbs
Eccl	Ecclesiastes

Song	Song of Solomon
Isa	Isaiah
Jer	Jeremiah
Lam	Lamentations
Ezek	Ezekiel
Dan	Daniel
Hos	Hosea
Joel	Joel
Amos	Amos
Obad	Obadiah
Jonah	Jonah
Mic	Micah
Nah	Nahum
Hab	Habakkuk
Zeph	Zephaniah
Hag	Haggai
Zech	Zechariah
Mal	Malachi

New Testament

Matt	Matthew
Mark	Mark
Luke	Luke
John	John
Acts	Acts
Rom	Romans
1–2 Cor	1–2 Corinthians
Gal	Galatians
Eph	Ephesians
Phil	Philippians
Col	Colossians
1–2 Thess	1–2 Thessalonains
1–2 Tim	1–2 Timothy
Titus	Titus

Phlm	Philemon
Heb	Hebrews
Jas	James
1–2 Pet	1–2 Peter
1–2–3 John	1–2–3 John
Jude	Jude
Rev	Revelation

PREFACE

Why title a book *Rescue: God and Sin in the Old Testament*? God speaks to us spiritually through the Bible, but I am not always sure that I hear the spiritual significance of what I am reading. This uncertainty drove me to study the spiritual significance of rescues (also known as "deliverances") in the Bible. When I began to look at them, I quickly discovered that I could not analyze all of them within a single book, so I elected to "begin at the beginning" with case studies of spiritual rescues in the Old Testament, emphasizing the earlier ones, beginning with Noah. This book represents only a sampling of spiritual rescues in the Old Testament. The reader is encouraged to find and analyze others.

Some readers may be put off by my use of the King James Version of the Bible (KJV), otherwise known as the Authorized Version. I beg the favor of giving it another chance in these pages. Although I am not a scholar of Hebrew nor Greek, my experience has been that much of the time, the accuracy of the KJV has been unchallenged. The English language has flattened in meaning over the last 400 years to the point of extreme literality. Authors of a popular textbook in hermeneutics can declare without challenge that English words "generally have but one intended meaning in any given context." Such statements are as rigidly dogmatic as the claim that generally each passage in the Bible has four meanings.

When the King James Bible was written, the English language was still rich in multiple meanings and nuance, not just puns and word play. Three brief examples:

- Lot "lingered," he did not just "hesitate," when he fled Sodom. Lingering is not willful, whereas hesitation often is. The difference was significant for the salvation of his soul.
- Jonah was "fast asleep" in the hold of a ship when the ship met a storm. The captain woke him up to pray to God for salvation. Being "fast asleep" is neither a metaphor nor a symbol. It has two simultaneous, equally valid meanings, one physical, the other spiritual. This literary device is known as ambiguity.
- In the King's English of the early 17th Century, "I will" (as opposed to "I shall") implied a promise, not a future action. This distinction has since been lost except in contract law. Promises by God that depend on future actions by people are important in the Bible, because people have not always kept their part of the "contract."

The KJV has its flaws, and when it is inaccurate or accidentally unclear, I have not hesitated to use the New American Standard Bible (NASB) in its place; however, in other instances it suggests nuance and even multiple meanings. The culture in which it was composed was alive with subtlety and ambiguity.

Although a book may have a single author, no one writes a book without help. I would like to thank two of my "preacher" friends, Ronnie Ray and Miles Stutts, who gave me valuable feedback on my ideas early on. My daughter Rachel took time from her work as an artist and graphic designer to draw two maps for the book, which I deeply appreciate. My wife, Janelle, and my son, Andy, read the manuscript and offered many valuable suggestions along the way. Any errors are my own oversights, and I apologize for them.

1

WHAT IS A SPIRITUAL RESCUE?

When I was 13 or 14 years old, I learned what a rescue was. Two friends and I went sailing in a small boat on Lake Michigan, just off the shore near Northwestern University. Our boat wasn't much more than an over-sized surfboard with a sail. There was barely room for three people on it, so we were sure to get wet, but it was a beautiful summer day, we were dressed in cut-off jeans, tee-shirts and life-jackets, and we didn't care. We had not paid attention to the weather, which was about to change.

About a half-hour into our sailing adventure, a line of clouds approached from the west, and the wind started to whip up waves several feet high. We were no more than 100 yards from the shore when the storm hit. A particularly strong gust blew our little sailboat over, and we found ourselves hanging on to the sides of the boat in the middle of a squall.

We were helpless, but with life jackets on, we were not in any real danger until a powerboat came over to give us a tow. The water was rough, and wind made it difficult for the skipper to maneuver his boat. He turned the cruiser around and backed towards us. I saw the twin screws of his propellers lift out of the water as he tried to buck the wind and waves with his stern. Now we *were* in danger, not of drowning but of being ground up by his propellers! Sensing the danger, we waved him off, and he obliged. He needed to get out of the storm almost as badly as we did.

My dad had always taught me that if I was sailing and the boat turned over, to "stay with the boat, and someone will see you." Even experienced swimmers cannot measure how far they can swim. One can swim and swim towards shore and not get any closer because of the unfavorable wind and waves. In this situation, it is easy to become exhausted and even to drown. However, an upturned sailboat is buoyant, and a boat is easier for a rescuer to see than a person in the water. I reminded myself and my friends, "stay with the boat, and someone will see us." The water wasn't too cold for us, but the lake was very large, and we were being blown away from shore. I became scared again. Who would see us being blown out into the lake? How long would it take before we were missed? Would someone find us before dark?

Just then, we saw another boat approach us. It was a small cutter from the U.S. Coast Guard Station in Wilmette Harbor. As their boat approached us from the side, one of the sailors stripped off his shirt and dove in towards us. One by one he took us to the cutter until we were all on board, shivering from fear as well as from the cold. I could not stop shivering, even when we arrived (boat in tow) at the Coast Guard station. As I recall, I had bouts of shivering the whole car ride home, replaying what happened and what might have been. It wasn't until I talked with my mom that I was able to stop shivering.

DEFINITION OF A SPIRITUAL RESCUE

I learned from my experience that a rescue has two defining features. First, the person being rescued must be in a dangerous situation. Sometimes we think that we are in danger when we are only wishing to avoid danger, but in a dangerous situation the threat is palpable. We can *feel* it, and we become frightened. Now much older, I have felt myself in a dangerous situation only a few times, but one of those times was in that Lake during that storm. Second, the people rescued must be helpless. If people are able to get themselves out of a dangerous situation, then they have not been rescued. They have simply used their own resources to escape the danger. A more experienced set of boaters might have waited out the storm, righted their boat, and sailed back to shore. We were not that experienced, so we needed a rescue. That is what I learned that day as an adolescent on Lake Michigan, where I was in a situation which I could not escape, even with the help of my friends. Not only I, but we were all helpless. There was nothing that we could do except wait.

Combine a dangerous situation with the knowledge that there is nothing you can do to save yourself and you have the makings of a rescue—if someone else helps you out. To this day, I do not know for sure why the Coast Guard cutter showed up when it did, where it did. Maybe the other boat called in a report. Every time I think of this incident, I thank God for the U. S. Coast Guard. Most of us have had incidents that are similar at least in one way: We were in a dangerous situation and we were unable to save ourselves. We were in need of help, and someone came to our rescue.

Why tell this story in a book about the Old Testament? A spiritual rescue is just like a physical rescue, except that the rescue is from sin and the rescue is by God or one of His agents. Briefly, **a spiritual rescue is an escape from a spiritually dangerous situation that requires spiritual help.** The 'clear and present danger' is that at some point, everybody loses their right relationship with God. "For all have sinned, and come short of the glory of God" (Rom 3:23), and they need a spiritual rescue.

When we were children, we all had a right relationship with God (Matt 19:14), not because we were righteous but because we were innocent. At some point, we all have been tempted by sin. Temptation creates a spiritually dangerous situation. If we do not resist the temptation, we end up committing sin. At that moment, we fall from innocence, and as a result, we become alienated from God. Sound familiar? It should. This is my story, your story and the story of humankind all the way back to Genesis.

One of the first lessons taught in a biblical Hebrew class is that *adam* is the word for "man." The story of Adam ("man") is everybody's story as they grew up. When Adam and Eve sinned, "the eyes of them both were opened, and they knew that they were naked; and they sewed fig leaves together, and made themselves aprons" (Gen 3:7). Adam and Eve lost their innocence. They sought to hide themselves from God out of guilt and shame. Once we lost our innocence and our right relationship with God, we needed a way to escape guilt and restore that relationship, but we could not do these things by ourselves. Helpless and in a state of spiritual danger, we needed a spiritual rescue. In this book, we shall explore how in Old Testament times, a number of people found themselves in that situation, and what God or His agents did to help them out of it. Before we begin these explorations, however, we need to know a little more about what a rescue involves.

PROCESS OF A SPIRITUAL RESCUE

If we look at a rescue not simply as an event but as a process, we can begin to see that it has a few step-wise features. A rescue follows a general outline or procedure, which can be viewed from the perspective of the rescuer or of the rescued. Let's view it from the perspective of the rescued, because that is what I was in the Lake that day—rescued.

Trust or Belief

The first step of the process of being rescued is to trust the rescuer. The skipper of the powerboat who tried to help us actually made the situation worse because he could not control his boat in the wind and waves. That fact was all too obvious to us as he backed towards us, frightening us. Fear tends to drive away trust. We lost any trust that we might have had in him as the older owner of a bigger boat than ours, so we waved him off with a signal to stop doing what he was trying to do. If we could not trust him to control his boat, we did not want him to attempt to rescue us for fear that he might accidentally harm us.

What gave us trust in the Coast Guard was partly their reputation for successful rescues. Rescues are a large part of their mission, and from what we knew of the Coast Guard, they were very good at them. I noticed that the cutter did not close in on us bow first, nor did it turn around and back towards us. As it arrived, the cutter turned slightly to approach us from the side. We could see that the sailors knew what they were doing. Further, they did not try to pick us out of the water from their boat, but a sailor dove in the water to fetch us, one by one. As the swimmer arrived for each one of us, he told us to let go of our boat and relax. Everything we knew about the Coast Guard and everything they did inspired our trust in them to save us.

Another word for "trust" is *belief*. The *Oxford English Dictionary* defines "trust" as "a firm belief in the reliability, truth, ability, or strength of someone or something." We trusted the Coast Guard because we believed that they could save us from the dangerous situation in which we were helpless. We believed not only in the Coast Guard's reliability as rescuers but in the swimmer's ability to rescue us individually. We had to believe in the ability of the swimmer for us to let go of our boat! One by one we did, and the swimmer towed each one of us to safety.

A spiritual rescue requires some degree of trust or belief in God. If we were to draw a line segment with "unbelief" at one end and "obedient belief" at the other, we would have a continuous representation of belief with the end points as extremes. The state of a person's belief in God and His word tends to fall somewhere along this line. We can even divide the line in the middle to distinguish four states of belief, two at the extremes, and one on each side of the middle of the line. Let's briefly explore each one (see Figure 1).

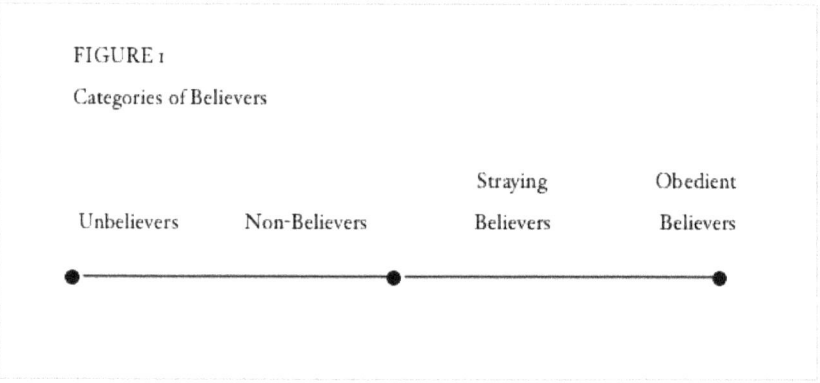

FIGURE 1
Categories of Believers

Unbelievers   Non-Believers   Straying Believers   Obedient Believers

Unbelievers. At one end of the line, "unbelievers" are people who consciously reject belief in the one true God and His word. "Unbelievers" may or may not be atheists. They may or may not belong to other religions and worship other gods. They may or may not call themselves "Christians." What they have in common is that they have heard or read the word of God, or they understand what is called *natural law* (Rom 2:14–15),[1] and they reject its truth. "Take heed, brethren, lest there be in any of you an evil heart of unbelief, in departing from the living God" (Heb 3:12). The Hebrew writer warned Christians not to abandon Christian beliefs and become "unbelievers" through their denial that there is only one true God and that His word is true.

Non-believers. A little more towards the center point of the line segment would be "non-belief." People who are non-believers neither accept nor reject the word of God as truth. They may or may not be agnostic. They may or may not have heard or read the word of God. What they have in common is that they are filled with doubt about it, or they have no opinion on the truth of God's word. They may worship other gods, but they neither believe nor disbelieve God and His word. They become unbelievers if they reject belief in God's word. They become obedient believers if they follow the commands of God consistently.

Straying believers. On the other side of the center point are people who trust in God and His word, and they have demonstrated their belief through an act of faith, but they are not following all of God's commandments under a governing covenant. They may consistently follow a few or many of them, but while straying believers, they fail to follow at least one of them. In short, they believe in God, but they are in sin. Their sin is not planned, willful or deliberate. If it were, they would be among "unbelievers," who reject the truth of God's word. Sometimes straying believers are said to sin out of ignorance, accident, or negligence. Straying believers need to become aware of their sin and repent. Once God has put their sin away, they become "obedient believers."

Obedient believers. At the other extreme from an unbeliever is the "obedient believer," who *believes* God, that is, who obeys Him consistently. The Old Testament used the terms "righteous" or "justified" for such a person. The New Testament writers preferred the terms "faithful" or "godly." Sometimes obedient believers in the New Testament are called "saints." Consequently, when Paul wrote to the Christians at Ephesus, and he addressed his letter to "the saints which are at Ephesus, and to the faithful in Christ Jesus" (Eph 1:1), he addressed people who were justified or righteous in the sight of God because they were obedient believers, doing the will of God.

Commands and Promises

In addition to our firm belief that the Coast Guard (and its swimmer) could rescue us, we had several commands to guide us. The most important one came from my father, who had always taught me to "stay with the boat, and someone will see you." I loved and respected my father, who had grown up on the shore of Lake Erie, and who had spent much of his early life boating on the Great Lakes. He knew what he was talking about. His command ("stay") came with the authority of experience, but it also came with a promise ("someone will see you") from his experience with boating accidents.

The other commands that I remember from the rescue came from the Coast Guard swimmer. He told each of us in turn to "Let go of the boat," then repeated to each of us: "Relax." I wanted to help him swim to the cutter, but any movement of mine only interfered with what he was trying to do, which was to swim with a sidestroke and hold me with his other arm across my chest. He needed me to relax so that he could swim evenly while keeping both our heads above water. I could not relax, but I stayed as still as possible while he towed me through the water. I am sure that to him, it felt as if he were towing a log.

When a rescue is on-going, the people being rescued often do not know what to do to be saved. Rescuers practice what they do; people being rescued do not, unless they have been drilled (lifeboat drill, fire drill, etc.). Consequently, many people being rescued are confused as well as frightened. Their efforts to save themselves may even put the rescuer in danger. A rescue swimmer, for example, may not be able to coax or pry them off their boat; the swimmer may be pulled under water by someone who does not know how to swim; the swimmer may be accidentally hit or choked by someone who has panicked. At a minimum, people being rescued probably have never been in this situation before. If they had, they might have known how to help themselves out of it.

Commands to people being rescued communicate information with verb form that allows the information to be transformed easily into action. The grammatical term for this verb form is "the imperative mood," which implies a second-person subject ("you"): "[You] stay with the boat." "[You] let go of the boat." "[You] relax." Rarely are commands explained. In a rescue, commands rely for their authority on a trust in the rescuer by the people being rescued. The trust that I had in my father, the trust I had in the Coast Guard, and the trust I had in the swimmer made my task of following commands easier, even if I had difficulty relaxing. I did not have to think about why I was doing what I was doing in order to be saved.

Commands vary in grammatical form in the Old Testament, but English translation of Hebrew has put most of them in the imperative mood, that is, most state the necessity that "you" do something.[2] The Ten Commandments, for example, are all in the imperative mood. They either state or imply the subject "you" (or "thou"). Instructions are also generally in the imperative mood; consequently, commands and instructions are grammatically equivalent, and when sequenced, they form a procedure. God's instructions in the Old Testament are often in the form of simple procedures, such as "Arise, go to Nineveh, that great city, and cry against it" (Jonah 1:2). The commands are "[You] arise," "[you] go" and "[you] cry." Failure to obey any or all of the divine commands within a set of instructions constituted sin.

Assurances sometimes accompany commands in the form of promises. When my dad taught me to "stay with the boat, and someone will see you," he provided me with a command and an assurance ("and someone will see you"). We do not think about it much, but the future tense in English has two forms that are unequal. If one were to say "I shall," it simply expresses the future, but if one were to say "I will," this alternate form of the future adds emphasis and implies a promise. A *promise* is defined as "A declaration or assurance that one will do a particular thing or that a particular thing will happen" (*Oxford English Dictionary*). The grammatical distinction between a simple statement of the future ("I shall") and a promise ("I will") is illustrated in Table 1. Note that this rule reverses terms in the second person (you) and third person (he/she/it/they).

TABLE 1

Biblical Uses of *Shall* and *Will*: Future, Promise and Commands

Future		Promise	
I shall	We shall	I will	We will
You will*	You will*	You shall*	You shall*
He, She, It will	They will	He, She, It shall	They shall

*commands

We no longer hold to this rule of prescriptive grammar, especially in everyday speech (e.g., my father did not follow it), but it is at least as old as Early Modern English, which was the language of Shakespeare and the King James Bible.[3] In that day, the translators of the Old Testament used it to distinguish promises from simple statements about the future. Consequently, when God commanded Abraham to "Get thee out of thy country, and from thy kindred, and from thy father's house, unto a land that I will shew thee" (Gen 12:1), the translators interpreted God's statement about the future ("*will* shew thee" instead of "shall shew thee") as an unfulfilled *promise*, not simply a statement about what was going to happen.

That is a handy tool for interpretation, because one soon discovers many promises in the Bible that are not obvious in most modern versions.[4] When in the last chapter we look at how promises function in the Old Testament, the conclusion will have the support of many examples. God did not make only a few promises in the Old Testament. He made hundreds of them, especially when belief was weak.

Obedience

Commands are meant to be followed, but they are not always obeyed, even in a rescue. I look back with a smile at the swimmer's command to "relax." All I could do was stay still. As soon as I was lifted out of the water, I found myself going through bouts of shivering. I was experiencing shock, but also the day had grown cooler with the passage of the weather front, all my clothes were wet, and the cutter was moving briskly towards its harbor. I was thankful when someone handed a blanket to me in which to wrap myself. The command to "relax" to me was as difficult to follow as the command to a child to "go to sleep." By staying still and shivering from time to time, I did the best I could to follow it.

To follow commands exactly as they are given is to do our part in the rescue. Most rescues have a part for the person being rescued, whether it is to follow a detailed procedure as in the evacuation of a building, to call on someone for help ("dial 9-1-1"), or just to wait or be still. One of the most difficult commands to follow is, "wait." In a dangerous situation in which we are helpless, we desperately want to do something to get out of it, but sometimes the best thing we can do is wait until help arrives. We have all heard about rescues that failed because the people who were to be rescued could no longer be found. They left the scene, hoping to rescue themselves, and as a result, they perished. "Stay with the boat" was a particular version of "wait." Believe me, it is a difficult command to obey when the safety of the shore seems close and you are moving farther and farther away from it.

People sometimes wait for a rescue on their own terms. These personal terms are often driven by expectations based on past experience. They are looking for something or for someone in particular to help them out of a dangerous situation. Frankly, the last thing that we boys expected was a rescue by the Coast Guard. We were looking for a passing boater, or even someone on the shore. We had no idea that the only cutter at the station was coming for us. The next day, I read in the *Chicago Tribune* that many sailboats in a race near Chicago had been blown over by the storm. Undoubtedly, they helped each other out of danger, but we were sailing alone. Who would guess that we would be the ones who perhaps needed a rescue most, and that we were the ones pulled out of the water most quickly. Rescues do not occur on our own terms. They do not necessarily follow our expectations. The people rescued are the ones who need to adapt to the conditions of the rescue, sometimes including waiting and watching.

In terms of a spiritual rescue, obedience to commands is the same. The rescue will fail if we disobey the instructions for the rescue. "But God be thanked, that ye were the servants of sin, but ye have obeyed from the heart that form of doctrine which was delivered you. Being then made free from sin, ye became the servants of righteousness" (Rom 6:17–18). The instructions for spiritual rescue have always included God's commands, which are meant to correct the sinner. Disobedience to these instructions means rejection of God's means of correction. We may or may not have another chance.

At a minimum, the process of a rescue requires the rescued person to trust the rescuer, to receive commands for what to do as part of the rescue, and to follow these commands exactly as they are given. The process of a spiritual rescue seems to parallel the process of a physical rescue, step by step. For the purposes of this set of case studies, the process of a spiritual rescue requires someone in danger to trust or believe in God or His agents, then receive commands for the rescue, then follow the commands obediently. Most spiritual rescues succeeded; a few failed. Both successful and unsuccessful rescues from sin are explored among the case studies presented in this book.

With a definition of a spiritual rescue and a description of its process as a tool of analysis, we can study spiritual rescues in the Old Testament for what they have to tell us about God's will for mankind. "For whatsoever things were written aforetime were written for our learning, that we through patience and comfort of the scriptures might have hope" (Rom 15:4). At the time that Paul wrote, "Scripture" included only the Old Testament, which he saw as profitable for giving hope. "Hope" was a confident expectation. There is every reason to believe that this series of case studies will furnish the reader with hope in the present life and for the hereafter. I am convinced that both Jews and Christians in the first century often saw the Old Testament in the light of spiritual rescues because of their needs for rescue both from their own transgressions and from societies that persecuted them. In particular, early Christians saw examples in Scripture of both what to do, and what not to do, to be rescued by God from sin.

A NOTE ON METHOD

Case study is a method of investigation in which an individual (such as a person, an organization, event or phenomenon) can be analyzed in light of some idea for the purpose of better understanding the individual *and* the idea. The idea in a case study represents a framework for analysis of the individual. This framework is tentative. It corresponds to an hypothesis in a scientific investigation. Whereas the goal of a scientific investigation is the discovery of cause-effect relationships through experimentation (or systematic testing of an hypothesis), the goal of case study is improved understanding of an idea and the individual person, organization, event, or phenomenon. Case study may reveal cause-effect relationships, but it does not manipulate them as an experiment does. It is a common method of investigation in both the social sciences and in business management where experimentation is sometimes problematic.[5] What is new in this book is the use of case study to shed light on a series of individual phenomena in the Bible and on the idea of a spiritual rescue.

The idea of a spiritual rescue itself is not new. In the King James Version of the Old Testament, spiritual rescue is sometimes called "deliverance" but more often called "salvation." To be rescued spiritually is the same as to be "saved" from sin, always by a divine intervention of some kind. In *The Divine Rescue,* Edward Fudge viewed the Old Testament as a prefiguration of God's rescue of the faithful from sin. The divine rescue occurred through the person of Jesus

Christ, who died for our sins, "that whosoever believeth in him should not perish, but have everlasting life" (John 3:16).[6] *The Divine Rescue* looked at God's overarching plan of rescue from Genesis to Revelation, whereas this book looks at only a selection of "smaller" spiritual rescues in the Old Testament.

Case study is likely to be unfamiliar to students of the Bible. The closest type of religious inquiry to a case study is a character study, in which a figure in the Bible such as Moses, Mary or Abraham is described, usually in terms of his or her virtues. An example of a set of character studies for adults is *Twelve Ordinary Men*,[7] in which the disciples chosen by Jesus are described as the title suggests, ordinary men. It is not a set of case studies, however, because "an ordinary man" does not provide a framework for analysis, only a point of departure for understanding the extraordinary transformation of these men into Apostles.

Case study methods have been applied to events in the Bible, but these events have not—so far—included spiritual rescues. An interesting application of case study method has recently been made to describe criminality in the Bible. *Criminals of the Bible*[8] uses twenty-five case studies of criminality including figures from both the Old and New Testaments. The purpose of the book was to understand better specific crimes described in the Bible as well as what the secular concept of "crime" is.

Methods of case study vary widely from the very formal to very informal. In these case studies, I have chosen to be informal, largely because of limitations in the data sources. Case studies generally focus on contemporary events, while case studies from the Old Testament focus on events well over two thousand years old. Multiple data sources of the kind expected by science are not available to describe events so far back in history. "Triangulation of data," which is a staple method of case study (borrowed from physical surveying), is not a technique conducive to the study of Scripture. However, multiple sources *within* the Bible provide opportunities to understand phenomena through a combination of perspectives, a concept known as *complementarity* (borrowed from physics).[9] The story of the exodus was told by Moses through the Book of Exodus, but critical details come to light in the Book of Ezekiel, which was not written by Moses; consequently, we have two contrasting perspectives, both inspired, that can and should be combined for a better understanding of the exodus. David's spiritual rescue was told through 2 Samuel, but it also appears to have been told through a series of Psalms (6, 38, 51, and 32). David wrote these psalms, but he did not write 2 Samuel; again, we have two contrasting perspectives, both inspired, that provide a better understanding of David's sin and repentance than either perspective alone. Many times, the Bible provides more than one perspective of the same event, providing opportunities for complementarity.

Case study always lifts an event out of context, however, so the reader or a teacher needs to provide some background knowledge. The cases of spiritual rescue that I have chosen assume a basic knowledge of Old Testament stories. This knowledge can be provided by independently re-reading sections of the Bible or by a teacher. Teaching by the case study method further assumes that students are familiar with the case. Some embarrassing moments for the student can be avoided if the teacher artfully works in the details of the case either by beginning with a review of the Old Testament story, or for more experienced teachers, by using the end-of-chapter questions to structure the lesson from the beginning, working in details of the case as they go. Either way, the subject of the book and its method of inquiry are not designed for an introductory class. They are designed for anyone with a basic knowledge of Old Testament stories and with a curiosity to learn more about rescues from sin and their meaning for Christians today.

STUDY QUESTIONS

1. Have you ever been physically rescued? Think about a) what made the situation dangerous and b) what made you feel helpless in it.
2. What was your role in being rescued? What were you expected to do to allow your own rescue to be completed?
3. What does it mean to be "rescued" from sin? Again, think about a) what makes the situation spiritually dangerous to the person being rescued, and b) what makes them helpless in it.
4. What is a sinner's role today in being spiritually rescued? What is the sinner expected to do to complete their rescue by God from sin?
5. What makes a case study different from a character study? Name at least one character in the Old Testament who became involved with sin. Was this person rescued by God? (Some are, some are not.) What were the consequences of being rescued, or of not being rescued?

2

RESCUE FROM AN EVIL WORLD

Noah

And God saw that the wickedness of man was great in the earth, and that every imagination of the thoughts of his heart was only evil continually (Gen 6:5).

We all know the story of Noah and the ark—or do we? We might have been taught in childhood that Noah was rescued from the flood, but if as adults we think carefully about what a rescue involves we come to a more accurate answer. Had Noah not built the ark, true, he would have drowned; but once he built the ark, he had a way to escape from a wicked world. Noah was not only rescued from death by drowning in the flood but from a wicked world through the flood. How do we know this "double rescue" to be true? We can look first to the Old Testament story of the flood for evidence of two rescues, not just one, then we can look to the New Testament for supportive evidence, in which several references are made to the Genesis flood. The evidence points to a spiritual rescue (from a thoroughly wicked world), as well as a physical rescue (from drowning).

The first thing that we learn about Noah other than his ancestry and his name is that he lived in a degenerate world:

> And God saw that the wickedness of man was great in the earth, and that every imagination of the thoughts of his heart was only evil continually. And it repented the Lord that he had made man on the earth, and it grieved him at his heart. And the Lord said, I will destroy man whom I have created from the face of the earth; both man, and beast, and the creeping thing, and the fowls of the air; for it repenteth me that I have made them (Gen 6:5–7).

Wickedness was not only everywhere, but people had corrupted their own minds to the point where they could only imagine doing what was wrong in the sight of God. Instead of following God, people followed their own lusts.

Mosaic law did not yet exist, but "natural law" did. Natural law, which was set by God, who made all things and declared them good, has always been the law by which Gentiles were guided without the laws of Moses (Rom. 2:14–15). Natural law respects the purpose or designed end of things. What is lawful conforms to its purpose, and what is unlawful violates that purpose. As a guide, mankind has an innate sense of right and wrong that comes from his creation in the image of God. Mankind knows to do what is lawful, but "the imagination of man's heart is evil from his youth" (Gen 8:21), so beginning in early adolescence, his moral guidance is mentally contested.

Mankind's corruption (by following the imagination of his mind rather than his sense of right and wrong) led God to "repent" or change His mind about what He had created. "And God said unto Noah, The end of all flesh is come before me; for the earth is filled with violence through them; and, behold, I will destroy them with the earth" (Gen 6:13). Here we see God make a vow or promise ("I will" rather than "I shall") to destroy all flesh, which must have been frightening. After all, Noah was "flesh" too.

About as close as we can get in the Bible to a detailed description of Noah's world is Paul's description of what society will be like just before the end of the time:

> For men will be lovers of self, lovers of money, boastful, arrogant, revilers, disobedient to parents, ungrateful, unholy, unloving, irreconcilable, malicious gossips, without self-control, brutal, haters of good, treacherous, reckless, conceited, lovers of pleasure rather than lovers of God, holding to a form of godliness, although they have denied its power (2 Tim 3:2–5 NASB).

Paul described such a time as "perilous" or dangerous. The danger was spiritual because of the temptations to approve, to participate in, or even to react in self-destructive ways to the ungodliness of a thoroughly corrupt world.

Not only was Noah spiritually at risk, but he was unable to escape using his own resources. He could not move away from evil, as a person might escape an evil ruler or a wicked society today by moving to another city or by emigrating to another country. Wickedness ruled everywhere, and "the earth was filled with violence" (Gen 6:11). There was nowhere safe from evil, even in the animal kingdom. Further, Noah's efforts to preach righteousness (2 Pet 2:5) persuaded no one to repent. He could improve his situation neither by changing locations nor by changing minds. His own resources could not help him. He was helpless and in need of a spiritual rescue from an evil world filled with unbelievers, who would not follow natural law.

The second thing that we learn about Noah is that he found "grace" in the sight of God. Noah's upright character, especially in a world full of evil, had something to do with God's unmerited favor. "Noah was a just man and perfect in his generations, and Noah walked with God" (Gen 6:9). His blamelessness in the sight of man and God not only allowed him to walk with God in fellowship, but it contrasted with the shamefulness of those whose thoughts were "only evil continually." They must have shunned him or mocked him. Noah was righteous, or what today we might call "faithful."

Noah demonstrated his faith by following a set of commands that were instructions for building a boat large enough to hold two animals of every kind. We know it as the ark. If Noah followed these commands, then he, his family, and representatives of the animal kingdom would have a means to escape an evil world:

> Make thee an ark of gopher wood; rooms shalt thou make in the ark, and shalt pitch it within and without with pitch. And this is the fashion which thou shalt make it of: The length of the ark shall be three hundred cubits, the breadth of it fifty cubits, and the height of it thirty cubits. A window shalt thou make to the ark, and in a cubit shalt thou finish it above; and the door of the ark shalt thou set in the side thereof; with lower, second, and third stories shalt thou make it (Gen 6:14–16).

The instructions were framed as a set of commandments or imperative verbs, with "thou" or "thee" either stated or implied. Following these commands was not presented as an option. It was *the* way out of the situation. What is striking about the commands is their specificity, down to the type of wood and the exact dimensions of the ark.

So far, God had given Noah only one promise ("I will destroy") but ten commandments (instructions for building the ark). Then God said a very curious thing: "But with thee will I establish my covenant" (Gen 6:18). This declaration was the second promise ("I will") made to Noah. The exact terms of the covenant were not specified.

Some people have tried to make this covenant into what is known as the "Rainbow Covenant." This second covenant, which was made after the flood had receded, was between God and every creature:

> And I will establish my covenant with you; neither shall all flesh be cut off any more by the waters of a flood; neither shall there any more be a flood to destroy the earth. And God said, This is the token of the covenant which I make between me and you and every living creature that is with you, for perpetual generations: I do set my bow in the cloud, and it shall be for a token of a covenant between me and the earth (Gen 9:11–13).

The "Rainbow Covenant" differs in several keys ways from the covenant with Noah. First and most obviously, it was made with every living creature, not just Noah. Second, it was highly explicit in its terms. Third, it was unconditional; that is, it did not require anything from creatures, including man. God promised for all time not to destroy all animal and human life with a flood. Neither man nor animal had to fear that rain would be a prelude to inescapable destruction. The rainbow was a perpetual sign of God's promise not to destroy the world again through water.

If the covenant between God and Noah was not some short form of the Rainbow Covenant, then what was it? We need to be careful here, because we do not want to add anything to the Bible, but at the same time, we do not want to miss any of its meaning. A covenant is between at least two parties and represents their promises to each other. The two parties of the first covenant were God and Noah, not God and all life. The context immediately before the covenant was a promise made by God: "And, behold, I, even I, do bring a flood of waters upon the earth, to destroy all flesh, wherein is the breath of life, from under heaven; and every thing that is in the earth shall die" (Gen 6:17). The context immediately after the covenant was a list of commands for who and what Noah was to include in the rescue from death: "Thou shalt come into the ark, thou, and thy sons, and thy wife, and thy sons' wives with thee. And of every living thing of all flesh, two of every sort shalt thou bring into the ark" (6:18–19). The list included all living things to be rescued, including Noah's immediate family.

If we use the context before and after the first covenant as our guide for interpretation, the implied content of the first covenant was an agreement to rescue Noah from an evil world and its destruction [God's part], if he would obey God's commands to build, load, and unload the ark [Noah's part]. It could have been as simple as, 'If you will be faithful [future], then I will rescue you from sin and death [promise].' Staying faithful would require Noah to follow the commands of God to build and load the ark before the flood and to unload the ark after the flood. As for God's part, he would rescue Noah from a sinful world and from drowning. If there were such an agreement, it would explain the "double rescue" noted at the beginning of the chapter. By building the ark as commanded by God, Noah created the means not only to escape an evil world but the means to escape being drowned by the flood.

The two types of rescue (spiritual and physical) were simultaneous for Noah, so they might appear to be the same, but they were not. Spiritual salvation was from sin. Physical salvation was from death. The promise of the covenant must have been to rescue Noah from both sin and death because that is what God did.

By following the many commandments to build the ark, Noah passed a test of obedience: "Thus did Noah; according to all that God commanded him, so did he. And the Lord said unto Noah, Come thou and all thy house into the ark; for thee have I seen righteous before me in this generation" (Gen 6:22–7:1). Presumably "this generation" was the period of time that Noah took to build the ark. The long period over which God tested Noah's obedience provided evidence of Noah's faithfulness. It also provided evidence of the unbelief of people in the old world. We already understand that Noah was "a preacher of righteousness," but more specifically, we are told by Peter that while "the ark was a-preparing," and while "the long-suffering of God waited," Noah preached to the disobedient in the spirit of Jesus Christ (1 Pet 3:19–20). What was that spirit? "I am not come to call the righteous, but sinners to repentance" (Matt 9:13). Noah repeated in some form God's promise to destroy them if they did not repent of their disobedience to what they knew was right (by their innate sense of right and wrong). They heard righteousness preached, but they rejected its truth. Their persistent unbelief led not only to their drowning but to their condemnation—the imprisonment of their souls in Hades to await judgment for their deliberate sins (1 Pet 3:19).

Much later, the writer of Hebrews interpreted Noah's obedience to the commands to build the ark in the same way—as a demonstration of faithfulness. Sometimes we forget that rain had never fallen on the earth before. The land had always been watered by dew (Gen 2:6). "By faith Noah, being warned of God of things not seen as yet, moved with fear, prepared an ark to the saving of his house; by the which he condemned the world, and became heir of the righteousness which is by faith" (Heb 11:7). Noah believed God with a conviction strong enough to sustain the construction of a huge boat over a lengthy period of time. His preparations were based neither on what he had seen nor on his ability to reason but on what he was commanded to do and out of fear of the promise God had made to destroy mankind. The degree of faith demonstrated by his obedience was sufficient for him to be called "righteous" or faithful, the same quality attributed to Abel and Enoch before him (Heb 11:4-5); therefore, Noah became "heir" of their righteousness. He was an obedient believer.

The Hebrew writer tells us that Noah built the ark "to the saving of his house," which meant that he wanted a rescue not just for himself, but for that part of his family which lived with him. These "eight souls were saved by water" (1 Pet 3:20) from an evil world, suggesting that the covenant between God and Noah covered not just Noah, but his wife, his three sons and their wives as well. This situation allowed for obedient children (and their obedient wives) to be saved from the evil of the ancient world, for more hands to care for the creatures on the ark, for companionship after the flood and for humankind to procreate from three younger pairs. We are not told why they were included with God's covenant with Noah, but they were. The covenant included not just Noah, but also his family, which was the genesis of all humankind.

The next question is, would Noah remain obedient to God *during* the rescues? If he did, a covenant with him such as 'If you will be faithful, I will rescue you from sin and death' would assure that if Noah remained obedient, God would complete the rescues. God laid out His commands to be obeyed during the rescues as a further set of instructions. They were as specific as the commands to build the ark, but their aim was different. They were instructions for the rescues themselves, or for Noah to do his part in the rescues.

Noah was obedient to the instructions and fulfilled his part. The evidence is abundant: "Thus did Noah; according to all that God commanded him, so did he" (Gen 6:22). "And Noah did according unto all that the Lord commanded him" (Gen 7:5). "Of clean beasts, and of beasts that are not clean, and of fowls, and of every thing that creepeth upon the earth, there went in two and two unto Noah into the ark, the male and the female, as God had commanded Noah" (7:8–9). Noah did everything that God commanded him to do, and he did it in the way that God commanded for it to be done.

We easily overlook that the covenant which God made with Noah, whatever it might have been, continued both during and after the flood. The rain lasted forty days and nights, the ark floated on the water, and "all flesh died that moved upon the earth" (7:21). Both human and animal life outside the ark was destroyed as God said it would be in His promise. After 150 days, "God remembered Noah, and every living thing, and all the cattle that was with him in the ark: and God made a wind to pass over the earth, and the waters asswaged" (Gen 8:1). Bruce Waltke has noted that the Hebrew verb for God to "remember" (*zakar*) "signifies to act upon a previous commitment to a covenant partner."[1] The statement that "God remembered Noah" is a figure of speech called an *ellipsis*. "God remembered [the covenant with] Noah" would be a full statement of its meaning. God kept His promise to rescue Noah from sin and death as He returned the ark and its contents to dry ground through His miraculous intervention ("God made a wind to pass over the earth"). He completed both the spiritual and physical rescues that He agreed to provide to the "heir of faith."

Noah's obedience did not end when the ground dried. Note the repetitions within the following passage. They represent a parallel between what God commanded before the door opened and what Noah obediently did to let the creatures out:

> And God spake unto Noah, saying, Go forth of the ark, thou, and thy wife, and thy sons, and thy sons' wives with thee. Bring forth with thee every living thing that is with thee, of all flesh, both of fowl, and of cattle, and of every creeping thing that creepeth upon the earth; that they may breed abundantly in the earth, and be fruitful, and multiply upon the earth. And Noah went forth, and his sons, and his wife, and his sons' wives with him: Every beast, every creeping thing, and every fowl, and whatsoever creepeth upon the earth, after their kinds, went forth out of the ark. (Gen 8:15–19)

This passage contains an internal parallel (or repetition) for a simple reason: After God completed the rescue, Noah continued to do exactly what God commanded him to do to unload the ark. His obedience to God's commands for unloading the ark mirrored his obedience in loading it. Noah continued to act from an obedient faith as he built an altar, sacrificed extra animals brought for that purpose, and worshipped God. The altar, sacrifice and worship confirm to us that Noah continued to act through faith. At least for a while longer, he remained an obedient believer.

The next question is, if God covenanted with Noah, what happened to the covenant? Did it dissolve when Noah worshipped God after the flood? Most people believe it covered only one family and one event. But what if the covenant with Noah were only an example of a "double rescue?" What would other "double rescues" in the Bible signal? The answer is some sort of relationship between the spiritual rescue and a physical rescue. The possibility exists that this relationship existed before Noah, continued through the rest of Old Testament times, and even may exist until the end of time. For the faithful, a physical rescue may somehow be associated with a spiritual rescue. Perhaps it is best if we describe the "double rescue" as **a rescue of the faithful from sin and death,** with the understanding that the spiritual rescue and the physical rescue are related, and it all exists by the grace of God. Let's explore this possibility, that the covenant with Noah was just one instance of a rescue of the faithful from sin and death.

During Old Testament times, such a rescue might have applied to Enoch, who walked with God and who was taken from the ancient world without experiencing death (Gen 5:24). Noah, who walked with God (Gen 6:9), was equally rescued from sin and death. The rescue of the faithful from sin and death may have included any number of individuals who were righteous in the sight of God, that is, people who were obedient believers. "He hath shewed thee, O man, what is good; and what doth the Lord require of thee, but to do justly, and to love mercy, and to walk humbly with thy God?" (Micah 6:8). People other than Enoch and Noah have walked, are walking, and will walk "humbly with God," and may receive a rescue from sin and death.

In the Christian dispensation, this type of rescue would extend to all who hear the word of God, believe it, repent of their sins, confess Jesus as the son of God, are baptized for the remission of sins, and live faithfully.[2] Let's briefly explore the possibility that rescue from sin and death exists in the Christian dispensation, including today.

Perhaps as clearly as anyone, Paul suggested that a rescue from sin and death existed in his day. He wrote to the struggling Corinthians that

> There hath no temptation taken you but such as is common to man: but God is faithful, who will not [future] suffer you to be tempted above that ye are able; but will [future] with the temptation also make a ["the," NASB] way to escape, that ye may be able to bear it (1 Cor 10:13).

God is faithful to fulfill a promise that He has made. Making *the* way of escape from temptation is that fulfillment. What was the promise for the faithful at Corinth? It was a promise of God to create a way for faithful Christians to escape temptation. The fulfillment of the promise was expressed by the King James translators as a future fact (God *will* create) rather than a promise. In other words, the creation of the escape route for the faithful was a future reality that they could depend upon, if they became helpless to escape spiritual danger on their own. The Christian's part was to remain faithful in obedience to God's instructions for the rescue—to follow *the* divinely created way out of temptation—just as Noah remained faithful in the way he loaded and unloaded the ark.

Paul's statement regards only the "first" of two rescues, which for Noah was the rescue from the temptations of an evil world. What about the "second" rescue, which is from death? In the same letter, Paul wrote to the Corinthians about a rescue from death when he wrote about the transformation of the physical body of each obedient believer on Judgment Day:

> So when this corruptible shall have put on incorruption [promise], and this mortal shall have put on immortality [promise], then shall be brought to pass the saying that is written, Death is swallowed up in victory. O death, where is thy sting? O grave, where is thy victory? The sting of death is sin; and the strength of sin is the law. But thanks be to God, which giveth us the victory through our Lord Jesus Christ (1 Cor 15:54–57).

When the world, which has become as corrupted as in Noah's

day, is finally destroyed, the faithful will be rescued by Jesus from what is mortal and corruptible. They are promised resurrection in a new, physical body that is not made of flesh and blood. That was Paul's vision of the physical rescue of the righteous, which was to follow the spiritual rescue from sin at baptism, and to follow repentance at any other time in life when they needed a way to escape temptation. In the Christian dispensation, God provides for both spiritual and physical rescues through Jesus Christ.

For Christians, temptations to sin today seem distant from the end of time—seemingly separating spiritual rescues today from the great physical rescue at the end of time—but that separation did not exist in the minds of early Christians, who faced temptations to sin in their daily lives and expected eternal judgment to occur soon. That separation should not exist in the minds of Christians today, either. Comparing the end of the world to the days of Noah, Jesus said,

> Heaven and earth shall pass away, but my words shall not pass away. But of that day and hour knoweth no man, no, not the angels of heaven, but my Father only. But as the days of Noe were, so shall also the coming of the Son of man be. For as in the days that were before the flood they were eating and drinking, marrying and giving in marriage, until the day that Noe entered into the ark, And knew not until the flood came, and took them all away; so shall also the coming of the Son of man be (Matt 24:35–39).

Jesus repeatedly promised his disciples and other listeners that the end of time was coming unexpectedly soon. This promise gave urgency to a Christian's spiritual rescue and nearness to a Christian's physical rescue. For obedient believers at the end of time, the two rescues—from an evil world (spiritual rescue) and from death (physical rescue)— will occur at the same time, just as they did in the days of Noah.

No active sinner (unbeliever, non-believer, or straying believer) will be rescued because there will be no time to repent. "We shall not all sleep, but we shall all be changed, in a moment, in the twinkling of an eye, at the last trump: for the trumpet shall sound, and the dead shall be raised incorruptible, and we shall be changed" (1 Cor 15:51–52). The rescue from death will occur at an unexpected time and "in the twinkling of an eye." There will be no opportunity for sinners to repent.

In the Christian dispensation, the part of the faithful believer in the first rescue is to keep to the way of Jesus Christ. To do so means to resist temptation by living like Christ. Paul described this requirement to the Philippians: "as ye have always obeyed, not as in my presence only, but now much more in my absence, work out your own salvation with fear and trembling. For it is God which worketh in you both to will and to do of his good pleasure" (Phil 2:12–13). Paul wrote these words to obedient believers. He similarly encouraged the Thessalonians (2 Thes 3:3–4). Faithful Christians are to be "blameless and harmless, the sons of God, without rebuke, in the midst of a crooked and perverse nation, among whom ye shine as lights in the world; Holding forth the word of life; that I may rejoice in the day of Christ" (Phil 2:15–16). The situations at Philippi and Thessalonica may not have been as desperate as that of Noah, but they clearly required Christians to resist temptation to sin "until the day of Christ" and a rescue from both a sinful world (a spiritual rescue) and from death (a physical rescue). In that day, Paul hoped to find them "Holding forth the word of life" or living in a godly manner as obedient believers.

There are other evidences of a rescue for the faithful from sin and death in the New Testament. Peter alluded to it when he wrote to the churches concerning false teachers. In his second letter, he warned of the dangers that false teachers presented: "through covetousness shall they with feigned words make merchandise of you: whose judgment now of a long time lingereth not, and their damnation slumbereth not" (2 Pet 2:3). Peter's description of the approaching destruction of unbelievers (i.e., false teachers) led him to describe the salvation of obedient believers, beginning with Noah. He concluded that "The Lord knoweth how to deliver the godly out of temptations, and to reserve the unjust unto the day of judgment to be punished" (2:9). Peter asserted that God had the power to rescue ("deliver") obedient believers ("the godly") out of temptations at any time, not just in the days of Noah. More particularly, he implied that God would rescue faithful Christians from the influence of false teachers, whenever their resources were insufficient to protect them. Eventually, God would provide Christians with the New Testament, so that they could use the written word of God to fend off unbelieving teachers, after the apostles and their students had died.

The general lesson that we can draw from Noah's rescue is that with Noah, God entered into a covenant or an agreement with a faithful person. Its terms are not specified in the Bible, but its context implies a promise of rescue from sin and death. If Noah continued to do God's will out of faith, God would rescue him from the temptations of the old world and from death by drowning during its destruction.

In the letters of Paul and Peter there is enough evidence of a rescue from sin and death for every Christian who is faithful to God's word to take comfort in it. Whenever they are in spiritual danger and helpless, Christians who are obedient believers have more than a chance for escape. God will [a future fact, not a promise] provide them *the* way out of the situation, if they continue to do His will and if they follow the instructions that are in the Bible. Further, by following the way of Jesus Christ until they die, obedient believers will also be able to overcome death. They will be rescued from sin in life and from death after life, if they remain faithful.

The means of rescue is best determined by God, whose hand "is not shortened, that it cannot save" (Isa 59:1). The way that He rescues may begin with obedience to His word, but it does not end there. If it did, many prayers of the faithful in times of need would go unanswered. Albert Barnes once commented, "He can send an angel to take his tempted people by the hand; he can interpose and destroy the power of the tempter; he can raise up earthly friends; he can deliver his people completely and forever from temptation, by their removal to heaven."[3] All of these forms of rescue took place in biblical times, and Barnes implied that all of them were possible in his day. Whatever our beliefs about the means God chooses to rescue the faithful, we must admit that He knows best how to conduct rescues from sin and death. He has been successfully about the business for a long, long time. Who are we to say what He can and cannot do?

Finally, a rescue for the faithful from sin and death is an idea that is worth consideration. Some bits of evidence in support of it have been provided, but it is far from proven. Nowhere in the Bible is it formatted as a principle of faith or even an explicit promise from God, but examples of double rescues (spiritual and physical) abound. That is what makes the case study of spiritual rescues so interesting. There is evidence that God has given Christians something quite wonderful to believe, even better than in the days of the Old Testament.

In the last chapter, the evidence for the idea of a rescue from sin and death will be summarized, then the reader can be the judge. Is the rescue of the faithful from sin and death a sentimental idea, or a special offer to select individuals, or a hope accessible to everyone who will be faithful? What does the Bible say when we listen to God speak spiritually?

STUDY QUESTIONS

1. What made the rescue of Noah spiritual? What made it physical? How did the condition of the world in the days of Noah pose a *spiritual* danger to Noah and his family? A

physical danger? Why was Noah helpless in the face of these dangers?
2. *If* a covenant with the faithful is in effect today, what would faithfulness require of us that it did not require in the days of Noah?
3. What *physical* rescue from a sinful world does God promise to the obedient believer today? Cite a verse in support of your answer.
4. Paul told the Philippians to "work out your own salvation with fear and trembling" (Phil 2:12). Explain why this advice does not mean "do whatever feels right to you" or "let your conscience be your guide."
5. Encountering a temptation, a faithful Christian might ask himself or herself, "What would Jesus do?" Refer to Matthew 4:1-11: Identify a temptation faced by Jesus, Summarize how Jesus responded, and Explain how His example serves as a model for us today.

3

RESCUE FROM SELF-RIGHTEOUSNESS

Job

So these three men ceased to answer Job, because he was righteous in his own eyes. Then was kindled the wrath of Elihu the son of Barachel the Buzite, of the kindred of Ram: against Job was his wrath kindled, because he justified himself rather than God (Job 32:1–2).

Most people say that the book of Job is about the suffering of a man who was "perfect and upright, and one that feared God, and eschewed evil" (Job 1:1), and it is (James 5:11), but there is another way to read the story. People who have argued that Job is righteous throughout his story tend to overlook what Job said about himself —and God—while defending himself against the accusations of his friends. He sinned while defending his righteousness. If we focus not on Job's suffering but on his rescue from the sin of self-righteousness, we gain insight into both how he sinned and how God used a man to rescue him from sin.

To understand Job's spiritual rescue, we need to review briefly Job's story. It begins with a meeting between God and Satan in heaven (before Satan and his angels were cast out). Like a hungry animal, Satan had been going "to and fro in the earth" and "walking up and down in it" (Job 1:7) , seeking someone whom he might tempt to sin. God asked Satan if he had "considered my servant Job, that there is none like him in the earth, a perfect and an upright man, one that feareth God, and escheweth evil" (1:8). Job headed a household with ten children and possessed large herds of livestock. He was "the greatest of all the men of the east" (1:3). Satan responded to God with the assertion that Job was faithful only because God had prospered and protected him. God allowed Satan to test the faithfulness of Job by allowing him to afflict Job with the loss of his possessions and his children, then with the loss of his health. Job's response was to mourn his terrible losses, but he remained faithful. Even though his wife urged him to "curse God, and die" (Job 2:9), "In all this did not Job sin with his lips" (2:10). Job did not give up his faith in God, but he did wonder why as an obedient believer, he suffered.

Job's weakness lay in his belief that he could not lose his righteousness. Some people today have a similar belief about their salvation. They become obedient believers when they become Christians. Without much further study of the Bible, they assume that the status of their belief cannot change, whatever they say or do. Once they are saved, they consider themselves always saved. Satan took advantage of a similar false belief by Job. Three friends came to Job "to mourn with him and to comfort him" (Job 2:11), "So they sat down with him upon the ground seven days and seven nights, and none spake a word unto him: for they saw that his grief was very great" (2:13). Only when Job opened his mouth and cursed the day that he was born did they begin to reply.

First one, then another of his friends accused him of sin. They believed that one way or another, his sins had caused his suffering. "Even as I have seen," said one, "they that plow iniquity, and sow wickedness, reap the same" (Job 4:8). They all believed that Job's suffering was God's punishment for sin. They denied that he had been obedient, and they spoke to him as if he were a straying believer.

Was Job a straying believer? Job asked to be taught what his sin was, but all that he received was a series of false accusations. "Teach me, and I will hold my tongue: and cause me to understand wherein I have erred" (Job 6:24). They did not succeed in teaching him what his sin was, so he did not remain silent. Rather, Job complained about his suffering, and sadly for him, he began to challenge God. "I will say unto God, Do not condemn me; shew me wherefore thou contendest with me. Is it good unto thee that thou shouldest oppress, that thou shouldest despise the work of thine hands, and shine upon the counsel of the wicked?" (Job 10:2–3). By promising to speak to God as he did, Job implied that God was oppressive, despiteful, and unjust. Job sinned with his words. Defending his righteousness in the way that he did, he fell from righteousness and became a straying believer, unconscious of his own sin.

What had happened? Satan had laid a clever trap by using Job's friends as accusers. Job was innocent of sin until he began to respond to the false accusations. Job assumed that he could remain righteous in defense of his righteousness. Anyone who has ever been falsely accused can identify with the anger that Job must have felt. Sadly, some of that anger was directed at God, and unknowingly, Job sinned by accusing God as he did. Job had strayed from the truth, but not in the way in which his friends had accused him, and not in a way of which he was aware. As a straying believer, Job was in spiritual danger, and he was helpless to escape on his own because he was unaware of his sin. Job was in need of a spiritual rescue.

After several rounds of accusation by Job's friends and self-defense by Job, Elihu spoke up. Who was Elihu? As "the son of Barachel the Buzite, of the kindred of Ram" (Job 32:2), Elihu was a young man from the town of Buz, which was named after the second son of Nahor, a brother of Abraham ("the kindred of Ram"). In Hebrew, *Elihu* literally means "my God is He," which labeled

Elihu as a believer in Jehovah God: He is my God. Elihu's father was named "Barachel," which means "God blesses," suggesting that belief in God ran in the family. The description of Elihu's ancestry is so specific in terms of faith that one has to wonder if he did not have another connection with God. The nature of this connection is at first unclear, but Elihu was thoroughly human. He was neither an angel nor a manifestation of Jesus Christ. Elihu was a young man with a special connection to God that would be revealed in time.

Elihu did not join with the three friends in their accusations against Job. Adam Clarke commented on his just character: "Elihu, better acquainted with human nature and the nature of the Divine law, and of God's moral government of the world, steps in, and makes the proper discriminations; acquits Job on the ground of their accusations, but condemns him for his too great self-confidence, and his trusting too much in his external righteousness."[1] In short, Clarke saw Elihu as just, Job's friends as unjust, and Job as having sinned only during his defense. Job had been innocent until he defended himself against his accusers.

As Clarke suggested, the underlying metaphor is a criminal trial. We are all familiar with the elements of a trial. There is a prosecutor, a defendant, a defendant's lawyer, and a judge. The prosecutor accuses the defendant with charges of a crime; the defendant's lawyer answers or responds to the charges, and the judge decides whether to acquit the defendant of the charges, or to find the defendant guilty. Metaphorically speaking, Job's friends were the prosecutors, accusing Job of committing a crime (i.e., a sin). Job was the defendant, but he made the mistake of defending himself. Until Elihu came along, he had no one except himself to defend him. In his anger and self-righteousness, Job claimed that the Judge had been unfair, as if the Judge were on trial. Elihu came into the picture as a lawyer, familiar with natural law, who was appointed by the Judge to defend Job after Job accused the Judge of unfairness. Job had unknowingly committed the 'crime' of what today we might call 'contempt of court.' A self-righteous person is generally unaware that he or she has been contemptuous of authority.

Elihu was neither a manifestation of God nor the judge in this "trial," but like the Judge, he was familiar with natural law and the order of things, including how a trial should proceed. "Behold," Elihu proclaimed to Job, "I am according to thy wish in God's stead: I also am formed out of the clay. Behold, my terror shall not make thee afraid, neither shall my hand be heavy upon thee" (Job 33:6–7). Job had no reason to fear Elihu's judgment of guilt or aquittal because Elihu had no power to punish or forgive. In giving his opinion, Elihu would act as a defense lawyer: An interpreter of the law seeking justice and mercy for his client.

Adopting the persona of Job, Elihu summarized Job's self-made defense against the accusations of his friends: "I am clean without transgression, I am innocent; neither is there iniquity in me. Behold, he findeth occasions against me, he counteth me for his enemy, He putteth my feet in the stocks, he marketh all my paths" (Job 33:9–11). Elihu's summary incorporated many of Job's own words from his earlier defense, including the self-righteous accusations against God. Job considered God to be like a man opposed to him ("he counteth me for his enemy"), but Elihu reminded Job that God was not a man, nor was it Job's place to contend with Him as he had done with his accusers. "Why dost thou strive against him? for he giveth not account of any of his matters" (33:13). Man should not contend with God because as man's judge, God is greater than man and does not have to account to man for his decisions.

Elihu had summarized for Job an explanation of what Job's sin was. Now he explained his own role to Job, and why Job should listen to him. Elihu explained that God communicates in various ways that cannot be interpreted by man without help. These means of communication included "in a dream, in a vision of the night" (Job 33:15), which was a reminder of what Job said earlier about God: "When I say, My bed shall comfort me, my couch shall ease my complaint; then thou scarest me with dreams, and terrifiest me through visions: So that my soul chooseth strangling, and death rather than my life" (7:13–15). Without an interpreter, the dreams that God gave to Job in his suffering only frightened him to the point of wanting to die. By himself, Job could not understand God when He spoke through dreams. He needed an interpreter.

God's means of communication also included corrective punishment:

> He is chastened also with pain upon his bed, and the multitude of his bones with strong pain: So that his life abhorreth bread, and his soul dainty meat. His flesh is consumed away, that it cannot be seen; and his bones that were not seen stick out. Yea, his soul draweth near unto the grave, and his life to the destroyers (Job 33:19–22).

The expectation of physical death was the same as that experienced by Job and a reminder to Job of what he lamented: bone-piercing pain (30:17), loss of appetite (3:24), loss of weight (16:8), and bones protruding from the flesh (19:20); in short, a physical wasting away. Without an interpreter, Job could not understand the meaning of his physical suffering.

Elihu did not interpret Job's dreams or physical suffering, but Job began to understand who Elihu was. He was an interpreter of the will of God. Similarly, Elihu understood Job's sinful frame of mind, so he reminded Job that repentance was an important part of restoring a right relationship between a person and God: "He [God] looketh upon men, and if any say, I have sinned, and perverted that which was right, and it profited me not; He [God] will deliver his [man's] soul from going into the pit, and his life shall see the light" (Job 33:27–28). Elihu gave Job a description of how repentance worked. Let's look at each part of this important statement (see Table 2).

TABLE 2

PROCESS OF REPENTANCE IN THE BOOK OF JOB

Process of Repentance	Interpretation
Admit guilt, e.g. "I have sinned" or equivalent	Recognize and communicate that one has sinned
Describe sin, e.g. "I have perverted that which was right" or equivalent	Understand and communicate what the sin is that was committed
Be penitent, e.g. "It profited me not," or equivalent	Feel and show regret for having sinned

Interestingly, the description of repentance is not in the imperative mood, suggesting that it was not prescriptive. It was not a set of commands to be followed as in a procedure but a model to be interpreted to suit the situation of the sinner. The model is specific enough, however, to suggest what sinners could say to repent. The words might include 1) an admission of guilt (e.g., "I have sinned"), 2) a description of the sin (e.g., "perverted that which was right"), and 3) being penitent (e.g., "it profited me not"). The process of repentance meant that sinners recognized that they had sinned; understood what their sins were; and felt and showed regret for having sinned. Christians today might find this description of the process helpful.

Elihu also gave Job a brief account of God's response to repentance, which restores righteousness to a straying believer. In the statement above, Elihu explained that God rescues ("will deliver") the repentant sinner from condemnation (for sin), and He promises that the repentant sinner will receive life ("his life shall see light"). Rescue from condemnation is a *spiritual* rescue, whereas rescue from death to life is a *physical* rescue. God's response to repentance was a rescue of the faithful from sin and death. Elihu's statement can be summarized: 'If a man will repent of his sins, God will rescue him from sin ["the pit"] and death ["his life will see light"].

Obedient belief, established by repentance, provides the foundation for God's completion of a rescue from sin and death.

Elihu had summarized Job's sin, explained that he was an interpreter of God's law, and described what Job needed to do to repent and what God's response would be. Did Job learn from what Elihu had just told him? Did he take the message to heart? Elihu said,

> Mark well, O Job, hearken unto me: hold thy peace, and I will speak. If thou hast anything to say, answer me: speak, for I desire to justify thee. If not, hearken unto me: hold thy peace, and I shall teach thee wisdom (Job 33:31–33).

Elihu challenged Job to refute ("answer") what he said, but Job remained silent. Job's silence was evidence of his willingness to "understand wherein I have erred" (Job 6:24). Job was willing to apply what he learned to himself. He was listening to Elihu—his advocate and the interpreter of God's will—and ready to learn.

Elihu had provided Job with all the information that Job needed to repent. Now he began persuasive arguments for repentance with a reminder that Job and his friends were to do the right thing.

> Hear my words, O ye wise men; and give ear unto me, ye that have knowledge. For the ear trieth words, as the mouth tasteth meat. Let us choose to us judgment: let us know among ourselves what is good. For Job hath said, I am righteous: and God hath taken away my judgment (Job 34:2–5).

Elihu reminded his audience that they had the power of choice, suggesting that not only Job but his friends needed to consider whether or not they needed to repent. He briefly described Job's sin again: Job claimed that God was prejudiced against him. With this brief prologue, Elihu set up a defense of God, and his main argument was that all men need to repent of their sins, especially Job.

His defense of God began with the argument that God will not act wickedly (Job 34:10–15). His characteristics are impartiality (34:16–20), omniscience (34:21–22), omnipotence (34:24–25), and omnipresence (34:26–29), all qualities of the ideal Judge. In response to corrective punishment, man should always repent. "Surely it is meet to be said unto God, I have bourne chastisement, I will not offend any more: That which I see not teach thou me: if I have done iniquity, I will do no more" (34:31–32). Elihu's point was this: When a person feels chastised or punished for an unknown reason, they can always turn away from doing whatever they are doing, even if they do not know what their sin is. In time, God will teach them, if they listen to the words of God and do not try to justify themselves. "he will recompense it, whether thou refuse [to repent], or whether thou choose [to repent]; and not I: therefore speak what thou knowest" (34:33). Elihu suddenly offered Job an opportunity to speak what he knew about his sin or in a word, repent, so that God could respond appropriately. Job remained silent, but Elihu had just told him what he sin was: "Job hath said, I am righteous: and God hath taken away my judgment" (34:5). What held Job back from admitting that he had sinned, describing his sin, and confessing its worthlessness?

Our legal system distinguishes between a crime that involves a high degree of intentionality from a corresponding crime that involves a low degree of intentionality. The root of such distinctions is divine law. Using the trial metaphor, Elihu began to accuse Job of a high degree of intentionality, or what might be called rebelliousness.

> Job hath spoken without knowledge, and his words were without wisdom. My desire is that Job may be tried unto the end because of his answers for wicked men. For he addeth rebellion unto his sin, he clappeth his hands among us, and multiplieth his words against God (34:35–37).

This new level of sin—rebellion—implied rejection of God and

His word, or as we have called it, unbelief. If we continue to use the metaphor of a trial, the accusation against Job changes from contempt of court (often unintentional and a misdemeanor) to obstruction of justice (an intentional crime and a felony).

At this point, one wonders if Elihu was trying to frighten Job into repentance. As far as we know, Job had neither "clapped his hands" to interrupt the trial, nor had he "multiplied his words" to Elihu by way of lengthy excuse. In fact, Job had become silent. Earlier with his friends, Job had sinned repeatedly. He had boasted about his righteousness (Job 35:2), doubted the advantage of his righteousness to God (35:3), and questioned whether there was any reward for repentance (35:3), but all of these sins were done in ignorance that he was sinning, not out of intention to sin.

Once Elihu had told Job accurately what his sin was and had informed Job about what to do to repent and be rescued from sin and death, the time for silence was over. Now was the time for Job to repent. If he did not repent, he could no longer claim ignorance of his sin because Elihu had just described it to him in words that were both unmistakably clear and prophetic of God's description of it. He would be in rebellion—an intentional sin—if he did not repent.

By God's design, the clouds which were over the heads of this little group were building. A storm was coming up, and Elihu began his closing argument. He told Job to observe nature, see how it revealed God's hidden knowledge, then glorify God. "Remember that thou magnify his work, which men behold. Every man may see it; man may behold it afar off" (Job 36:24–25). The greatness of God's work could be observed through rain falling in the distance.

> Behold, God is great, and we know him not, neither can the number of his years be searched out. For he maketh small the drops of water: they pour down rain according to the vapour thereof: Which the clouds do drop and distil upon man abundantly (36:26–28).

Elihu urged Job to consider God's knowledge in the formation of rain, and more generally, in the storm that was approaching. "Also can any understand the spreadings of the clouds, or the noise of his tabernacle?" (36:29). God's knowledge was not only magnified by the rain and clouds swelling towards them, but in the mysterious rumble of approaching thunder as His voice. Elihu wanted Job and his friends to be awed and even frightened by the approaching and boundless knowledge of God in contrast with what little they knew.

Elihu confessed to Job and his friends that he was moved by the storm's display of God's knowledge and power. "At this also my heart trembleth, and is moved out of his place" (Job 37:1). Elihu encouraged his listeners to feel the awesomeness of God. "Hear attentively the noise of his voice, and the sound that goeth out of his mouth (37:2). They could listen to the thunder, but Job and his three friends could not understand it. "God thundereth marvelously with his voice; great things doeth he, which we cannot comprehend" (37:5). With the storm nearly upon them, Elihu wanted Job to consider the incomprehensible wisdom of God in nature and silently, to contrast God's wisdom with his own ignorance of God's will and way of working. He wanted Job, the straying believer, to fear the approach of judgment. Then Elihu disappeared from the conversation.

Did Elihu fail to rescue Job? Only if that were his mission, which it was not. His mission appears to have been to inform Job of his sin and persuade Job to respond appropriately. If Job, by way of humbling himself and repenting, would become faithful again, then God would rescue him from sin and death. Elihu had prepared Job to respond to God with humility, rather than angrily or defiantly.

A terrifying "whirlwind" or tornado developed out of the thunderstorm. "Then the Lord answered Job out of the whirlwind, and said, Who is this that darkeneth counsel by words without knowledge? Gird up now thy loins like a man: for I will demand of thee, and answer thou me" (Job 38:1–3). The storm that approached the little group broke over them, and "out of the whirlwind" came the voice of God to command Job to answer for his sin, identified by God as "words without knowledge," just as Elihu said. If Job remained silent, God would condemn him for disobedience to the command to speak. At the same time, the tornado threatened to consume and destroy Job and his friends.

No doubt the tornado, the sound of God's voice and the command to speak increased Job's fear. He did not utter a word in response while God questioned him: "Where wast thou when I laid the foundations of the earth? declare, if thou hast understanding" (38:4). Of course, Job did not know, and he remained silent. The fearful questioning by God continued, as did the silence of Job, until God demanded an answer: "Shall he that contendeth with the Almighty instruct him? he that reproveth God, let him answer it" (Job 40:2). As a straying believer, Job either had to repent of sin now or he would be in rebellion along with other unbelievers. There was no room for hesitation.

Responding to God's demand to speak, Job said, "Behold I am vile; what shall I answer thee? I will lay mine hand upon my mouth. Once have I spoken; but I will not answer: yea, twice; but I will proceed no further" (40:4–5). Job admitted his sinfulness ("behold, I am vile"), but his response was not complete repentance. To do his part in the rescue, Job needed to describe his sin and be penitent, as Elihu had informed him. He needed to follow through with repentance.

Because Job had not fully repented, God continued his questioning, now more narrowly directed at Job's sin:

> Then answered the Lord unto Job out of the whirlwind, and said, Gird up thy loins now like a man: I will demand of thee, and declare thou unto me. Wilt thou also disannul my judgment? Wilt thou condemn me, *that thou mayest be righteous*? (Job 40:6–8, emphasis added)

God's last question addressed Job's sin directly. God threatened judgment: "Hast thou an arm like God? or canst thou thunder with a voice like him?" (40:9). "Then will I also confess unto thee that thine own right hand can save thee" (40:14). Job knew that no one other than God could "save" or rescue a straying believer from sin and death. The whirlwind was almost upon him.

Job's only answer to God was full repentance. Job's words in the following passage are set normally, while his summaries of God's words are set in bold:

> I know that thou canst do every thing, and that no thought can be withholden from thee. **Who is he that hideth counsel without knowledge?** therefore have I uttered that I understood not; things too wonderful for me, which I knew not. **Hear, I beseech thee, and I will speak: I will demand of thee, and declare thou unto me.** I have heard of thee by the hearing of the ear: but now mine eye seeth thee. Wherefore I abhor myself, and repent in dust and ashes (Job 42:2–6).

Job had already admitted that he had sinned (Job 40:4). Now he continued His reply by continuing his repentance: He described his sin ("therefore have I uttered that I understood not"), and he was penitent, both feeling and showing regret for his sin ("wherefore I abhor myself, and repent in dust and ashes").

What just happened? Actually, two rescues of Job were under way. In the first one, God commanded Job to listen to Him, and He commanded Job to declare what he knew. These commands were sequenced for Job's rescue from self-righteousness. Job obeyed the commands by 1) repeating the words of God (in bold), to show that he had obeyed the command to listen; and 2) repenting of his sin of self-righteousness. After Job repented, God repeatedly called him "my servant," and He gave him the function of a priest to intercede for his friends through prayer. God spiritually rescued Job from sin, restoring his righteousness, but He also rescued Job from physical anguish and death.

In the second rescue, God freed Job's body from Satan's physical control. In the beginning, Satan had told God, "Skin for skin, yea, all that a man hath will he give for his life. But put forth thine hand now, and touch his bone and his flesh, and he will curse thee to thy face. And the Lord said unto Satan, Behold, he is in thine hand; but save his life" (Job 2:4–6). Job's dreams and body led Job to wish he were never born and to wish he could die. "And the Lord turned the captivity of Job, when he prayed for his friends: also the Lord gave Job twice as much as he had before" (Job 42:10). After Job repented, God's anger was appeased, the tornado miraculously disappeared, and Job saw "the light of life" shine on him.

We can see in the story of Job a rescue of the faithful from sin and death. This association would predict not only rescues from sin *and* death, but a rescue from sin *before* a rescue from death. That order of rescues is implied by rescues in which *God establishes faithfulness through obedience to commands for the spiritual rescue*. If Job had disobeyed either command for the spiritual rescue ("hear" and "declare thou unto me"), he would not have been justified or faithful in God's sight, and God would not have rescued him from death. That is why Job needed to demonstrate his faithfulness by repenting *before* he could be released from the captivity of Satan and *before* the life-threatening danger of God's anger could be appeased. He had to have his faithfulness restored before he could be included with the faithful in a rescue from death.

When viewed as a spiritual rescue from self-righteousness rather than as an example of extraordinary suffering and endurance, the story of Job has new meaning. From this angle, we discover more about what it means to be self-righteous. The very nature of self-righteousness is for someone to think that they know all the answers, when they don't. Only God does. A self-righteous person also thinks, 'I am right, and you are wrong,' without considering the truth of the matter or the limitations of their point of view. They lack humility. If they persist in their self-righteousness, they will never know the truth that will set them free from sin and death. They must follow the instructions for their spiritual and physical rescues exactly as they are given.

We also discover from Job that extraordinary suffering in life may be a sign that a person should stop saying what they are saying or doing what they are doing and carefully listen to God's word. That listening may come from reading the Bible, hearing a faithful interpretation of it, or both. It requires the listener to hear God spiritually. If Christians should find that they have sinned, the book of Job teaches what it means to repent—to admit sin, describe it, and both feel and show regret for their sins.

Finally, we see in the book of Job a rescue of the faithful from sin and death extend beyond Noah and his family. We discover that a straying believer could be rescued from death if he became faithful during a spiritual rescue. *He re-established his faithfulness by following the commands for a spiritual rescue.* In doing so, he not only became free from sin, but he found that "his life will receive light" rather than the specter of death. Ultimately, the message of Job is a message of hope for the unintentional sinner. It shows how faithfulness is lost through unintentional sin, but also it shows how faithfulness can be regained through humility and repentance.

STUDY QUESTIONS

1. Satan used Job's friends to tempt him to sin. Can you think of an example when friends might tempt someone to sin? What should the person do?
2. Elihu said that Job was "righteous in his own eyes." Why did Elihu become angry?
3. When did the spiritual rescue of Job begin? What made the rescue necessary?
4. Elihu provided Job with a model for repentance, and

God gave the commands that Job would have to obey to complete his part of the rescue. What were those commands from God, and what led Job to obey them?

5. Describe an example of a sin against God today (e.g., breaking a commandment given by Jesus to his followers) and what someone might say and do to repent of it.

4

RESCUE FROM DOUBT

Abraham, Sarah, and Hagar

> Then Abraham fell upon his face, and laughed, and said in his heart, Shall a child be born unto him that is an hundred years old? and shall Sarah, that is ninety years old, bear? (Gen 17:17)

We could discuss Abraham, Sarah and Hagar as three separate cases, but they are so intertwined in their stories and their stories have so many common elements that we may as well discuss them together. God chose Abraham, first known as "Abram," to father a nation that would be faithful to Him. This nation would descend from Abraham and his wife Sarah (first known as "Sarai"), who was his half-sister. Abraham would also become the father of another nation through Hagar, who was Sarah's Egyptian handmaid or servant. How these nations came to exist involved the rescues of Abraham, Sarah and Hagar from the same sin, which was doubt.

Abraham's father was named Terah, and like many others in his generation, Terah was an idolater. Later, Joshua would say to the people of Israel that "From ancient times your fathers lived beyond the River, namely, Terah, the father of Abraham and the father of Nahor, and they served other gods" (Josh 24:2 NASB). The land "beyond the River" Euphrates was Mesopotamia, a land full of idolatry. God called Abraham out of Mesopotamia to make a new people who would serve Him. Taking with him his father, his wife Sarah, and his brother Nahor, Nahor's wife (Milcah), and Lot (his nephew by a deceased brother), Abraham stopped in Haran, where God spoke with him again.

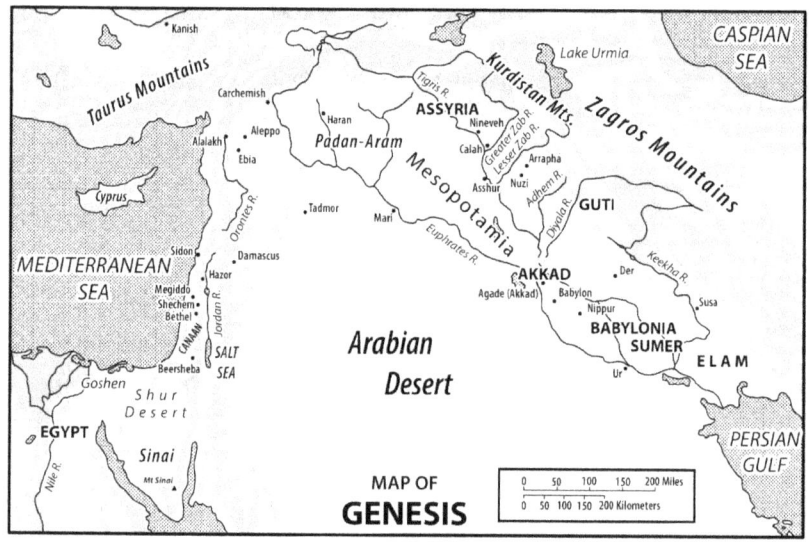

Leaving Mesopotamia and his family required more than belief in God. It required obedient belief, or *believing* God. In other words, leaving his home required Abraham to obey commands based on the authority of God. His obedience would not be without a reward, however, because of a promise:

> Now the Lord had said unto Abram, Get thee out of thy country, and from thy kindred, and from thy father's house, unto a land that I will shew thee: And I will make of thee a great nation, and I will bless thee, and make thy name great; and thou shalt be a blessing: And I will bless them that bless thee, and curse him that curseth thee: and in thee shall all families of the earth be blessed.

So Abram departed, as the Lord had spoken unto him; and Lot went with him (Gen 12:1–4).

God's second call was almost identical to his first call, but He added "from thy father's house" to the conditions for receiving the promised blessings. Abraham's father would die in Haran, and his brother Nahor and his wife would settle near there. On the basis of faith in the promises, Abraham, Sarah, and their nephew Lot would continue the journey to "a land that I will shew thee," which we know as Canaan, or the Promised Land.

At the foundation of Abraham's faith was the promise of a homeland (the 'land' promise) and a promise to make a "great nation" from him (the 'seed' promise). God promised to make his reputation great, bless those who blessed him, and extend his influence through his children to bless all nations. What made Abraham's belief in these promises extraordinary was the age of his wife Sarah. He was 75 when he left Haran (Gen 12:4), and she was 65. They had no children. All the promises by God had to be fulfilled through the children of Abraham, who were as yet unborn. For these promises to be fulfilled, Sarah would have to bear children in old age, or Abraham would have to find a new wife.

Ten years passed, but still no child was born. Abraham was 85 and Sarah was 75. The absence of a family heir to the promises (including the 'land' promise) was beginning to shake the foundation of Abraham's faith. Abraham must have wondered, how could God's promises be fulfilled if he had no children? "And Abram said, Lord God, what wilt thou give me, seeing I go childless, and the steward of my house is this Eliezer of Damascus?" (Gen 15:2). God promised a nation and land to Abraham's children, but childless, Abraham had only a steward to inherit the promises. "And, behold, the word of the Lord came unto him, saying, This shall not be thine heir; but he that shall come forth out of thine own bowels shall be thine heir" (15:4). God then showed Abraham the stars in the night sky and said "So shall thy seed be" (15:5). Even though Abraham could not see into the future, he believed God's promise ("So shall thy seed be"), and God "counted it to him for righteousness" (15:6). God attributed righteousness to Abraham based on Abraham's belief in the divinely promised future. Abraham was an obedient believer, so he continued in silence.

If God attributed righteousness to Abraham, why did Abraham need a spiritual rescue? What put him in spiritual danger? In a word, *doubt*. Since the flood, a new generation had been born every 30-35 years, casting reasonable doubt over the ability of Abraham and Sarah, both of whom had now lived to more than twice that age, to have children. More particularly, Sarah, who was 75 years old, was beyond natural child-bearing age. God confronted and corrected Abraham's doubts that led him to question God about Eliezer, but at the same time, He did not resolve the growing doubt in Sarah. She did not approach Him with her questions. Instead, she began to think about how she and Abraham might fulfill, on their own, what God had promised.

Apparently, Sarah thought that if the promises were to be fulfilled through an heir, the mother of the heir would have to be a younger woman. "Now Sarai Abram's wife bare him no children: and she had an handmaid, an Egyptian, whose name was Hagar" (Gen 16:1). Abraham, Sarah and Lot had visited Egypt earlier to escape a famine in Canaan, and Sarah probably received Hagar as a gift from an admiring Pharaoh. Hagar was Sarah's "handmaid" or slave. We can assume that Hagar was much younger than Sarah and therefore a reasonable candidate to be the mother of a child by Abraham. "And Sarai said unto Abram, Behold now, the Lord hath restrained me from bearing: I pray thee, go in unto my maid; it may be that I may obtain children by her. And Abram hearkened to the voice of Sarai" (16:2). Sarah's statement about the Lord ("Behold now, the Lord hath restrained me from bearing") implied that she had passed the age of menopause. Her plan was reasonable, but it was also sinful because it supplanted God's role in the fulfillment of His promises to Abraham.

Abraham's compliance with Sarah's plan was based on reasoning and experience rather than on faith. Abraham knew that his father, Terah, was old when he began to have children (Gen 11:26), and he must have agreed with Sarah's conclusion that the cause of their childlessness was in her rather than in him. A child conceived by Hagar from his seed would literally be from his own "bowels" (inner body), and therefore, her child by him would (he thought) be an approved means to fulfill God's promise to him.

Scheming like this only undermined his faith in God to fulfill His promises. Reasoning and experience led Abraham to conclude that together with his wife and her servant, he could create a way for God to fulfill His promise to him. He did not trust God to find the way for him to have a child. Both Abraham and Sarah sinned by doubting God, but neither sinned willfully nor on purpose. They were believers who strayed from obedient belief, but they were not unbelievers.

Sarah went so far as to arrange a marriage between Abraham and Hagar (Gen 16:3). Apparently because of a custom, Sarah believed that she could claim as her own the child of her husband's marriage with her slave. The marriage itself was not sinful, as men at that time and in that culture could have several wives, but the plan to conceive an heir to inherit the promises was sinful because it circumvented God's will. "And he went in unto Hagar, and she conceived: and when she saw that she had conceived, her mistress was despised in her eyes" (Gen 16:4). The only results were a baby and strife.

Hagar was at first an innocent and even abused party, but she lost her innocence when she thought herself better than Sarah, and violated the natural order of the home:

For three things the earth is disquieted, and for four which it cannot bear: For a servant when he reigneth; and a fool when he is filled with meat; For an odious woman when she is married; and an handmaid that is heir to her mistress (Prov 30:21–23).

Hagar sinned against natural law when she saw herself as "heir to her mistress," thinking of herself as Abraham's new and better wife because she was young and bore his child.

Sarah wished that Abraham felt Hagar's distain in order to prompt him to resolve the matter. "And Sarai said unto Abram, My wrong be upon thee: I have given my maid into thy bosom; and when she saw that she had conceived, I was despised in her eyes: the Lord judge between me and thee" (Gen 16:5). Sarah wished that she could transfer Hagar's disdain for her to him so that Abraham could know how she felt and do justice. Abraham did justice by transferring Hagar to Sarah's authority: "Behold, thy maid is in thy hand; do to her as it pleaseth thee" (16:6). Abraham essentially gave Hagar back to Sarah, likely ending the cohabitation but not the marriage to Abraham, which would last 13 more years.

Hagar became Sarah's handmaid again, but Sarah dealt so harshly with her that Hagar ran away into the desert. In Hebrew, *Hagar* means "flight." She was in flight from Abraham and Sarah, but earlier, she had also fled with them from Egypt when Pharaoh discovered that Sarah was Abraham's wife. "And the angel of the Lord found her by a fountain of water in the wilderness, by the fountain in the way to Shur" (16:7). Evidently, Hagar, feeling mistreated by both Abraham and Sarah, was on her way back to Egypt, but she had stopped by a well before crossing a desert named *Shur*, which means "wall" in Hebrew. It is a natural barrier between Egypt and nations to the northeast. For a pregnant woman on her own, it represented a formidable obstacle.

She could not assume a friendly welcome back in Egypt because of the conditions under which Abraham and Sarah departed. Where was she to go? Her physical dilemma—whether to try to cross over the desert into Egypt or to return to Abraham and Sarah—reflected a spiritual dilemma of where to look for guidance. She had stopped before attempting to cross "the wall," and as a pregnant, run-away slave on her own and without a plan, she was undoubtedly in great distress.

There are a several clues that Hagar was a non-believer. She was an Egyptian, and at one time, she probably worshipped Egyptian gods; she did not turn to God for physical guidance or spiritual comfort, even in distress, but she did not reject him either; and she had never been viewed as the spiritual equal of Abraham or Sarah. God would approach her through the angel of the lord, but his approach was not evidence of her being godly. God has always found a way to approach sinners (e.,g., Elihu in Chapter 3), either to warn them (unbelievers) or persuade them (non-believers), depending on the nature of their sin. As a non-believer, Hagar needed to be persuaded that God was her God, which is exactly what the angel of the Lord did.

The angel of the Lord approached Hagar to persuade her to believe in Him and to repent of her sin against natural law. In response to her distress, "the angel of the Lord found her" (Gen 16:7), "And he said, Hagar, Sarai's maid, whence camest thou? and whither wilt thou go?" (16:8). In either direction of Egypt or Canaan, Hagar faced a future with uncertainty and no guidance. She must have been surprised that the angel had approached her, knew who she was, and asked the question that she was asking herself ("whither wilt thou go?").

The angel put her dilemma in words, and she trusted him enough to reply with all honesty, "I flee from the face of my mistress Sarai" (16:8). She told him from where she had come, but she did not tell him where she was going because she did not know. "And the angel of the Lord said unto her, Return to thy mistress, and submit thyself under her hands" (16:9). The angel supplied her with physical and spiritual guidance through his commands, but she also needed to decide whether or not to believe him and follow his commands. She had not yet believed in God, let alone believed God. She was still a non-believer.

What tipped the balance in favor of believing the angel was what the angel did next. First, he promised her something that she believed she was owed from the promises made to Abraham: "I will multiply thy seed exceedingly" (16:10). The angel gave her a promise that was essentially the same as the "seed" promise that God gave to Abraham. Second, the angel told her that she would bear a son, "and [thou] shalt call his name Ishmael; because the Lord hath heard thy affliction" (16:11). *Ishmael* is Hebrew for "God Will Hear," which explained to her how and why the angel suddenly appeared to her. God heard her distress. Third, the angel foretold a particular future for her son. "And he will be a wild man; his hand will be against every man, and every man's hand against him; and he shall dwell in the presence of all his brethren" (16:12). The angel promised that although her son would be in conflict with his brothers, there would be a place for Ishmael and his descendants among them.

Hagar now became a believer in God. First, Hagar expressed her belief in the angel of the Lord and in God. "And she called the name of the Lord that spake unto her, Thou God seest me: for she said, Have I also here looked after him that seeth me?" (Gen 16:13). She named the angel "Thou God Seest Me" (*El Roi*) and she named after Him the well where He found her— *Beerlahairoi*, which means "The Well of Him that Lives and Sees Me." She believed in God because He saw her first, not only in her need for physical guidance ("whither wilt thou go?"), but also in her need for spiritual guidance, that is, guidance in whom to believe. Even today, we often honor people by naming after them a place where they did something significant or important for us. In this case, God saw and heard Hagar in trouble at the well, and through His angel, He persuaded her to believe in Him.

Did God spiritually rescue Hagar from sin? The answer is yes, but the first sin from which God rescued her was non-belief. Through a spiritual rescue which involved a persuasive demonstration of God's existence, presence and knowledge, Hagar became an obedient believer in God, intent on following His instructions. Her statement, "Have I also here looked after him that seeth me?" (16:13) was a rhetorical question that probably expressed her surprise at seeing God there. There is some debate about the translation,[1] but the context suggests a miraculous vision not just from God but of God as a reward for believing in Him and her decision to accept the guidance that He had already given to her ("return" and "submit") through His angel.

Did God rescue Hagar physically from death? The answer becomes clear as we consider her choices at the well. Had she continued towards Egypt, with or without a passing caravan, she had to cross *Shur*, a desert which was a formidable obstacle to Moses and the Israelites more than 400 years later when they came out of Egypt. The Israelites

> went out into the wilderness of Shur; and they went three days in the wilderness, and found no water. And when they came to Marah, they could not drink of the waters of Marah, for they were bitter: therefore the name of it was called Marah. And the people murmured against Moses, saying, What shall we drink? (Exod 15:22–24)

After three days' journey out of Egypt and into the Shur desert, they found no drinkable water. Further, had Hagar tried to join a passing caravan to Egypt, all kinds of dangers awaited her, the least of which was being sold, as Joseph was (Gen 39:1).

Had Hagar been caught as a runaway slave, or even had she returned to Sarah unrepentant, she could have suffered severe punishment. James B. Coffman summarized the conservative view: "She was engaged in an illegal flight, which, according to the laws of that age, could have been punished severely, even with death."[2] If so, Sarah could have let justice play out after Hagar gave birth, and Sarah could have had the newborn child all to herself. Hagar might have died either by attempting to cross the Shur desert in her condition (with or without a caravan), or by being caught and returned as a run-away slave. Either way, God rescued her from the prospect of death, suggesting that a rescue of the faithful from sin and death was in progress even before Hagar believed in God. After she believed, she demonstrated her faithfulness by obeying the commands of the angel of the Lord. Peace reigned in Abraham's family because the natural order of master, mistress, and handmaid returned.

After Hagar's son Ishmael was born, 13 years passed, and Abraham, Sarah, and Hagar all assumed during this time that God's "seed" promise would be fulfilled through Ishmael.

> And when Abram was ninety years old and nine, the Lord appeared to Abram, and said unto him, I am the Almighty God; walk before me, and be thou perfect. And I will make my covenant between me and thee, and will multiply thee exceedingly (Gen 17:1–2).

God then prophesied a fact about Sarah that revealed Abraham's faith was not perfect: "And I will bless her, and give thee a son also of her: yea, I will bless her, and she shall be a mother of nations; kings of people shall be of her" (17:16). Abraham's response was not "amen," but "Abraham fell upon his face, and laughed, and said in his heart, Shall a child be born unto him that is an hundred years old? and shall Sarah, that is ninety years old, bear?" (17:17). By laughing, Abraham revealed that he doubted that God could fulfill His "seed" promise through such a miracle. He expected God's promises to be fulfilled through Ishmael.

Abraham's laughter was neither deliberate nor derisive. It was impulsive and genuine. Abraham seemed unaware that his laughter revealed that he was a straying believer. Like Job, Abraham's ignorance of his own sin put him in spiritual danger and helpless to escape it on his own. Consequently, Abraham needed a spiritual rescue. He needed his belief in God strengthened to overcome doubt.

God came to his rescue with detailed promises, not commands. He began by sharing with Abraham a few details from His plan for salvation of the world: "And God said, Sarah thy wife shall bear a son indeed; and thou shalt call his name Isaac: and I will establish my covenant with him for an everlasting covenant, and with his seed after him" (Gen 17:19). God made three promises that revealed how He would make a great nation from Abraham. God promised that 1) Sarah would have a boy, 2) God would covenant with the boy, and 3) He would covenant further "with his seed." By further promising that "Sarah shall bear unto thee at this set time in the next year" (17:21), and by commanding Abraham to name his son Isaac, God gave Abraham sufficient details to persuade him to believe His promise of a son by Sarah.

For Abraham, repentance of doubt also required repentance of a false belief—that the "seed" promise to him would be fulfilled through Ishmael. God made a separate set of promises for Ishmael, which provided a prosperous future for him parallel to the promised future for Isaac. "As for Ishmael, I have heard thee: Behold, I have blessed him, and will make him fruitful, and will multiply him exceedingly; twelve princes shall he beget, and I will make him a great nation" (17:20). These promises served essentially the same purpose as the promises for Isaac. They increased the believability of the "seed" promise for Ishmael through credible details. They were persuasive.

Not long after God visited Abraham, He returned in the persona of three men who passed by Abraham's tent on their way to Sodom (Gen 18:1–2). Abraham immediately recognized them as a representation of God. "My Lord, if now I have found favour in thy sight, pass not away, I pray thee, from thy servant" (18:3). Abraham invited them to rest and take a meal. After their meal under a tree, they visited with him. Their first words were "Where is Sarah thy wife?" (18:9). Abraham responded that she was in the tent. What occurred next revealed the purpose of God's visit:

> And he said, I will certainly return unto thee according to the time of life; and, lo, Sarah thy wife shall have a son. And Sarah heard it

in the tent door, which was behind him. Now Abraham and Sarah were old and well stricken in age; and it ceased to be with Sarah after the manner of women. Therefore Sarah laughed within herself, saying, After I am waxed old shall I have pleasure, my Lord being old also? (Gen 18:10–12)

The information about Isaac's birth was not news to Abraham, and neither did he laugh. His failure to laugh or show any sign of disbelief suggests that he had been persuaded to believe God's promise of a son to him through Sarah. The purpose of God's visit to Abraham's tent was to persuade Sarah.

Sarah's response to the news was similar to Abraham's response when he first heard it. She laughed "within herself" and silently asked herself a question that further revealed her doubt about God's ability to fulfill His "seed" promise through her. At 89, she was beyond menopause ("ceased to be . . . after the manner of women") and almost as frail as her husband. The thought of having a baby seemed ridiculous. Her sin was not her laughter to herself, which was merely an expression of it. Her sin was her long-standing doubt that Abraham could have a son through her. Like her husband's doubt, her sin was unintentional.

God confronted Sarah with her sin to rescue her from sin. Sarah concealed the laughter in her heart, but God knew her heart, and at first, He spoke to Abraham within her hearing:

And the Lord said unto Abraham, Wherefore did Sarah laugh, saying, Shall I of a surety bear a child, which am old? Is any thing too hard for the Lord? At the time appointed I will return unto thee, according to the time of life, and Sarah shall have a son (Gen 18:13–14).

Although speaking to Abraham, God showed Sarah who He was by revealing to her what she thought only she knew: She had laughed to herself at the news that she was to have a son. God made two promises in her hearing: He would return at the time of birth, and her child would be a boy. Both promises added details to persuade her to believe in God's promise to her, that she would have a son (Gen 18:10).

Sarah impulsively lied to Him out of fear: "Sarah denied, saying, I laughed not; for she was afraid. And he said, Nay; but thou didst laugh" (18:15). God not only confronted her doubt about His power to work a miracle ("Is any thing too hard for the Lord?"), but He contradicted the lie that came from her fear. Sarah's doubt was fully exposed; she was certainly ashamed and afraid; then the brief visit with her ended. Apparently, God had persuaded her to believe in His promise because nothing is too hard for the Lord.

Paul sketched out the rest of Abraham's rescue including the renewal of his strength:

> Who against hope believed in hope, that he might become the father of many nations, according to that which was spoken, So shall thy seed be. And being not weak in faith, he considered not his own body now dead, when he was about an hundred years old, neither yet the deadness of Sarah's womb: He staggered not at the promise of God through unbelief; but was strong in faith, giving glory to God; And being fully persuaded that, what he had promised, he was able also to perform. And therefore it was imputed to him for righteousness (Rom 4:18–22).

We can put the renewed strength of Abraham on a timeline. He had repented of his doubt ("was strong in faith") that God would fulfill His "seed" promise through Isaac. In response to his strengthened faith, God ascribed righteousness to him, then *because of Abraham's righteousness*, God miraculously strengthened his body so that he could do his part in conceiving the child.

The book of Hebrews sketches out the rest of Sarah's story: "Through faith also Sara herself received strength to conceive seed, and was delivered of a child when she was past age, because she judged him faithful who had promised" (Heb 11:11). If we also put her renewed strength on a timeline, the sequence would be: 1) "she judged him faithful who had promised," that is, Sarah overcame her doubt with her decision to trust God to fulfill His "seed" promise; and 2) because of her faithfulness, God gave her the strength to conceive and bear a child, even though she was past the age of child-bearing. The strength to conceive and suffer through labor at her age was a miracle.

Given these interpretations of events, we can see how a rescue of the faithful from sin and death weaves its way into the story of Abraham and Sarah. As soon as Abraham's belief in the "seed" promise drove out his doubt of God's ability to fulfill it, he regained his faithfulness. The restoration of his faithfulness was the result of his spiritual rescue. His restored faithfulness then became the foundation for a second rescue, which was physical. The body of a 99 year-old man, which was "a body now dead," was rejuvenated in function, if not in flesh. This rejuvenation was a miracle, demonstrating an intervention by God. Had God not rescued Abraham physically through a miracle, Abraham would not have been able to perform what God required from him to conceive a child. That was a miraculous physical rescue from 'death.' The result was a rescue of the faithful from sin and death.

Through God's visit in the persona of three men, and the information that God gave her through them, Sarah was rescued from the sin of doubt. Once her faithfulness was restored, she was miraculously rescued from "the deadness of her womb" just as her husband was rescued from "his own body now dead." Their "dead" functioning came alive, and they were able to have a son. We know from God's promise to be there that He was an attendant at the birth.

Again, we have rather clear views of the relationship between the spiritual rescues and the physical rescues. The spiritual rescues freed both Abraham and Sarah from doubt, restoring their righteousness. Their righteousness *caused* their physical rejuvenation, which was both the effect of their righteousness and a miracle from God. The miracle was not just a signal of God's approval. It was functional. Without the miracle, Abraham and Sarah would not have had the strength to conceive a child on their own.

Abraham obediently named the child: "And Abraham called the name of his son that was born unto him, whom Sarah bare to him, Isaac" (Gen 21:3). *Isaac* is Hebrew for "he laughs." Every time that he heard the name of his son, Abraham would recall his own sin. The name meant the recollection of her laughter and more to Sarah: "And Sarah said, God hath made me to laugh, so that all that hear will laugh with me" (21:6). Isaac's name gave Sarah cause for mixed feelings, sorrow for her sin and joy for her child.

On the advice of Sarah, supported by God, Abraham "cast out" Hagar and Ishmael. Sarah promised Abraham that "the son of this bondwoman shall not be heir with my son, even with Isaac" (Gen 21:10). Apparently, Sarah believed in only one set of promises. In fact, during the 13 years between the birth of Ismael and his circumcision, everyone believed that Ishmael was heir to the promises of God to Abraham. Within a year after Ishmael was circumcised, God persuaded both Abraham and Sarah that Isaac would become heir of the promises, informing Abraham of a second, special set of promises for Ishmael (Gen 17:20), but Sarah and Hagar still believed in only one set of promises. That is why Sarah did not want Ishmael to share in the inheritance with Isaac. Even Abraham may have forgotten about these separate promises: "And the thing was very grievous in Abraham's sight because of his son" (21:11). Only Abraham was reassured that Ishmael would receive his own promises to become a nation (21:13).

The "thing" that was so grievous was divorce. The Hebrew word for "cast out" is *garash*, which means "to drive out from a possession; especially to *expatriate* or *divorce*" (*The New Strong's Concordance of the Bible*). Being "cast out" meant that Abraham divorced Hagar and disinherited Ishmael of Abraham's possessions, but it also meant that Hagar and her son were freed. They were no longer slaves of anyone. Further, conflict that was already developing in the home between the elder and younger sons would be avoided, at least for a time. As for Isaac, he would become the undisputed heir of Abraham. The divorce seemed to benefit everyone except Ishmael, who along with his mother must have wondered what he now possessed.

When she left with her son, all Hagar had was a bottle of water, bread, and a doubt that God would fulfill the promises made to her more than 13 years earlier about Ishmael. Had he been disinherited from the promises to Abraham because of the divorce? Now that Isaac had become sole heir to the "seed" and "land" promises, what was left for Ishmael except the promise of being wild and in conflict with mankind? Hagar apparently believed that Ishmael would inherit nothing of value, leading her to stray from her belief that God fulfills His promises. She sinned by doubting God.

The Bible tells us that with her son, "she departed, and wandered in the wilderness of Beer-sheba" (Gen 21:14), which today would be the Negev Desert. Her physical wandering was certainly a sign of her mental distress. "The water was spent in the bottle, and she cast the child under one of the shrubs. And she went, and sat her down over against him a good way off, as it were a bowshot: for she said, Let me not see the death of the child" (21:15–16). She sat far enough away from him that she would not have to see him die of thirst.

The angel of the Lord intervened to rescue Hagar both from sinful doubt and death in the desert. A voice from heaven commanded her to "Arise, lift up the lad, and hold him in thine hand; for I will make him a great nation" (Gen 21:18). This promise ("I will make him great nation") assured her that her son would be heir to a promise from God that was similar to the promise that Isaac would inherit. Ishmael would not inherit the promises to Abraham, nor would he be offered a covenant relationship with God (Gen 17:21), but Ishmael would be promised to become "a great nation," living a nomadic life among his brethren. The voice from heaven persuaded her to believe that God fulfills His promises.

A miracle allowed her to rescue her son from death. "And God opened her eyes, and she saw a well of water; and she went, and filled the bottle with water, and gave the lad drink" (21:19). She got up ("arise"), retrieving the bottle, going to the well, filling the bottle, returning to her son, lifting up his upper body ("lift up the lad") and holding up his head ("hold him in thine hand") as the best way to give a drink out of a bottle to a person too weak to sit up on their own. Again, we see evidence of a rescue of the faithful from sin and death: First, a rescue from the sin of doubt, then after her faithfulness was re-established, a miraculous physical rescue of both her and her son from death by dehydration. Her restored belief caused God to open her eyes so that she could see water and live.

In the cases of Abraham, Sarah and Hagar, we learn more about rescues of the faithful from sin and from death. God offered a spiritual rescue to a non-believer and to straying believers through persuasion. He approached the straying believer even before the believer knew that he or she strayed. He did not always give commands for the rescue, but he used other methods, such as promises and questions, to persuade straying believers to believe Him and repent of their sins. Once they did, they became obedient believers, and they were rescued from death by a miracle. *The miraculous physical rescue was a reward for their righteousness*. We can now see that at least in the Old Testament, the relationship between the spiritual rescue and the physical rescue was not a simple cause-effect relationship. The miraculous nature of the physical rescue gave God a presence and power in this relationship that made it both merciful (the rescue from sin) and gracious (the rescue from death).

God was also introduced as "El Roi," the God Who Sees. Nowhere else in the Bible is this name given to Him, but it points to a key characteristic of God. The angel of the Lord called Hagar; Hagar did not call for him. His presence near her at the well when she was a non-believer was an indication that even for non-believers, God is always near, and when a spiritual rescue is called for, He takes the initiative. Consequently, a rescue of the faithful from sin and death, which extended to Job as a straying sinner, also extended to Hagar as a non-believer. She had to repent of her non-belief to be rescued from sin, but once she was rescued from sin, she became an obedient believer and included among the faithful to be miraculously rescued from death. The central message of these rescues from doubt is there is hope for straying sinners in a rescue of the faithful from sin and death.

If Christians stray from the truth, and more particularly, if they doubt God's ability to fulfill His promises, they need to allow themselves to be taught using Scripture, and more importantly, taught to use Scripture. There are many reasons why people in contemporary society might doubt His ability to do what He says He will do. His promises do not always accord with contemporary expectations developed from experience or reason, but our role is clear. We are to love God and obey Him. One of the best ways for Christians to be convinced that God will do what He promises to do is to study what He promised to do in the Old Testament. There we see Him fulfill all of His promises for that time.

STUDY QUESTIONS

1. When did Abraham and Sarah begin to doubt whether or not God would be faithful to His promises? What caused their doubt? Why was it a sin?
2. Why did Hagar doubt that God would fulfill His promises for her son? What reassured her?
3. Why do people doubt God today? What spiritual danger does it pose for them? What can make them feel helpless to escape their doubt?

4. How do we escape doubt today? What increases our faith in God's word?
5. What part do the faithful play in the rescue of doubters? How can doing *their* part in spiritual rescue of others from doubt, allow God to rescue *them*? (Hint: 1 Peter 4:8)

5

FAILED RESCUE FROM UNINTENTIONAL SIN

Lot

> And while he lingered, the men laid hold upon his hand, and upon the hand of his wife, and upon the hand of his two daughters; the Lord being merciful unto him: and they brought him forth, and set him without the city. (Gen 19:16)

The story of Lot sits between two episodes in the story of Abraham and Sarah. The two episodes are strikingly similar: In the first, a famine drove Abraham and his household from Canaan into Egypt. Abraham deceived Pharaoh into believing that Sarah was his sister rather than his wife. Because Pharaoh attempted to add Sarah to his harem, God brought "great plagues" on him and his household until he repented (Gen 12:10–20). In the second episode, Abraham similarly deceived Abimelech, King of Gerar, into thinking that Sarah was his sister (Gen 20:1–18). Because Abimelech took her, God "fast closed up all the wombs of the house of Abimelech" (20:18) until he repented. The two stories sit like bookends for the story of Lot. Taken together, they suggest that we should pay attention to the subject of unintentional sin—the sins of Pharaoh and Abimelech— when we study the case of Lot.

"Lot's choice" today is synonymous with a selfish decision, but self-interest is not the same as selfishness. A more sympathetic interpretation of "Lot's choice" deserves a hearing, particularly because much later, the Apostle Peter had high regard for Lot before Lot sinned. Referring to the difficulty of Lot's life in Sodom, Peter twice referred to Lot as "righteous" and also as "just" (2 Pet 2:7–9). A sympathetic reading of "Lot's choice" should also find him righteous and just, at least at the beginning.

As Lot reached adult standing and responsibilities, Lot filled the role of his deceased father (Abraham's brother Haran). When Abraham's and Lot's herdsmen came into conflict, Abraham said, "Let there be no strife, I pray thee, between me and thee, and between my herdsmen and thy herdsmen; for we be brethren" (Gen 13:8). If we miss the significance of "we be brethren," we miss the high esteem Abraham had for his nephew, who stood in place of his brother, Haran. His high esteem may also have partly been due to a shared faith in God.

Abraham's esteem for Lot explains why Abraham gave Lot first choice of land on which to settle. It was a gracious act of an elder brother to a younger "brother." It appears that Lot returned the favor by choosing land that was not promised to Abraham by God. Lot's choice of land was beyond the eastern boundary of Canaan, which was the Jordan River.[1] Lot saw "the plain of Jordan, that it was well watered every where, before the Lord destroyed Sodom and Gomorrah, even as the garden of the Lord, like the land of Egypt, as thou comest unto Zoar" (13:10). Today, no one knows where most of the cities of the plain were, but they appear to have been southeast of Canaan, across the Jordan River and in or near what is now the Dead (or Salt) Sea. The surest separation of herds and herders would be by bodies of water, suggesting that Lot chose land that was both outside the borders of Canaan and across bodies of water that acted as a natural barrier to separate herds of cattle, goats or sheep.

The first lesson that can be learned from Lot's choice of land is that appearances can deceive. The plain may have brought to mind the Garden of Eden, but "the men of Sodom were wicked and sinners before the Lord exceedingly" (13:13). Lot may not have known the character of the people of Sodom when he "lifted up his eyes and beheld all the plain" (13:10). He may only have seen the best ground that had not been given by God to Abraham.

A second lesson to be learned from Lot's choice is that Lot was righteous and just, exactly as Peter described him. He decision to live in a land not promised to Abraham was righteous in the eyes of God because it conformed to God's will. Lot's decision to resolve any potential conflict by establishing a clear boundary between Abraham's herds and his own herds was just in the eyes of man because it caused "no strife" between the herdsmen.

Lot's righteousness in the sight of God and his reputation for justice with his fellow man did not exempt him from trouble. Lot was rescued not once but twice. His first rescue was by the hands of his uncle. The five kings of the five cities of the plain paid tribute money for twelve years to Chedorlaomer, the ruler of Elam, a kingdom much farther east. The Bible says, "in the thirteenth year they rebelled" (Gen 14:4). The next year, Chedorlaomer with three allied kings led a raiding party to punish the rebels "in the vale of Siddim" (14:3) which was near the plain of the Jordan. "And the vale of Siddim was full of slimepits; and the kings of Sodom and Gomorrah fled, and fell there" (14:10). As a consequence, the raiding party plundered Sodom and Gomorrah, also taking "Lot, Abram's brother's son, who dwelt in Sodom, and his goods, and departed" (14:12). Apparently, their intent was to hold Lot captive until ransomed, or use him as a slave, or both.

Lot needed a spiritual and a physical rescue. He was an obedient believer who became the captive of kings who served the pagan gods of Mesopotamia. Like Noah, he was surrounded by spiritual danger and helpless to escape on his own. Abraham heard of his capture, armed 318 of his own trained men, and strategically attacked the raiders at night and from different directions. The attack chased the raiding party out of the region, freed Lot, restored his goods to him, and brought back other captured people and stolen property after "the slaughter of Chedorlaomer" (14:17). The simultaneous spiritual and physical rescues were successful, and Melchizedek, who was the king of Salem (Jerusalem) and "priest of the most high God" (14:18), brought bread and wine to nourish the victorious men. Melchizedek blessed Abraham "and said, Blessed be Abram of the most high God, possessor of heaven and earth: And blessed be the most high God, which hath delivered thine enemies into thy hand" (14:19–20). The spiritual and the physical rescues occurred at the same time, signaling that even though he lived in Sodom, Lot was still righteous. God's deliverance of a victory (a physical rescue) over five kings was the miracle that rewarded his righteousness.

Lot's other rescue was more complex because it was led by the angels of God and it involved both temptation and sin. In Chapter 4, we saw how God in the form of three men visited Abraham's tent to confront Sarah's doubt. Upon leaving, He decided to tell Abraham about His plan for Sodom and Gomorrah:

> And the Lord said, Because the cry of Sodom and Gomorrah is great, and because their sin is very grievous; I will go down now, and see whether they have done altogether according to the cry of it, which is come unto me; and if not, I will know. And the men turned their faces from thence, and went toward Sodom: but Abraham stood yet before the Lord (Gen 18:20–22).

Both God and Abraham knew the "cry" or reputation of Sodom and Gomorrah was for wickedness. The source of their wickedness was their violation of natural law—those "unchanging moral principles regarded as a basis for all human conduct." Through angels, God would go down to Sodom to determine whether the practices of Sodom and her sister cities accorded with their reputation for violating natural law.

Both God and Abraham knew that Lot lived in Sodom. Abraham inferred that God might destroy Lot along with Sodom, so he began to negotiate to rescue him. "Wilt thou also destroy the righteous with the wicked?" (18:23). Eventually, God agreed to spare Sodom if as few as 10 righteous people lived there (18:32).

Later, God described what the sins of Sodom were. He said,

> Behold, this was the iniquity of thy sister Sodom, pride, fulness of bread, and abundance of idleness was in her and in her daughters, neither did she strengthen the hand of the poor and needy. And they were haughty, and committed abomination before me: therefore I took them away as I saw good (Ezek 16:49–50).

The people of Sodom and the other cities of the plain ("her daughters") prospered only to please themselves.

Many have wondered, what was Lot doing in Sodom? Lot was living in Sodom because he found protection, companionship, and business there. Essentially, the city fulfilled the function of his absent uncle, so much so that he would address its residents as "brethren" (Gen 19:7) even though they were related to him neither by blood nor by belief. Further, the people had given Lot some status in the city (perhaps as a result of the rescue by his uncle), allowing him to sit as a judge at their gate (19:1). This status met his need for esteem filled earlier by his uncle when he treated Lot as a brother. If all five cities of the plain were wicked enough to be destroyed with all their inhabitants, Lot did not have a better place to go on his side of the river to live.

If anything, Lot's situation in Sodom illustrates how difficult a godly life is in a thoroughly wicked place. Lot relied on the inhabitants of Sodom to meet his needs, but their ungodly lifestyle troubled him. Peter would later understand the situation. He wrote that Lot was "vexed with the filthy conversation of the wicked" (2 Pet. 2:7). By *vexed*, he meant troubled. By *conversation*, he meant interaction. Lot saw and heard disrespect of the natural laws of God: "For that righteous man dwelling among them, in seeing and hearing, vexed his righteous soul from day to day with their unlawful deeds" (2:8). Living in Sodom tortured Lot mentally, but moving to another city of the plain would not have offered him any greater peace of mind.

Two of the three men who had visited Abraham continued their journey to Sodom. They were messengers from God: "And there came two angels to Sodom at even; and Lot sat in the gate of Sodom: and Lot seeing them rose up to meet them; and he bowed himself with his face toward the ground" (Gen 19:1). The rescue of Lot and his family began as a parallel to God's visit to Abraham's tent, where Sarah was spiritually rescued. There were two instead of three men, it was evening rather than noon, and Lot was seated at the gate of the city rather than at the flap of a tent, but the unmistakable parallels suggest that we are to compare the two events.

Both Lot and Abraham responded to visitors with similar hospitality, offering them water to wash their feet, freshly prepared food, and a place to rest. Whereas Abraham recognized God's voice among his visitors, Lot did not recognize the men as angels; nevertheless, he treated them with honor by rising at their approach, bowing in their presence, and addressing them in terms of respect. "And he said, Behold now, my lords, turn in, I pray you, into your servant's house, and tarry all night, and wash your feet, and ye shall rise up early, and go on your ways" (Gen 19:2). Lot set the standard to "Be not forgetful to entertain strangers: for thereby some have entertained angels unawares" (Heb 13:2). His actions were exemplary even though he did not know who the men were. Comparing Lot's hospitality with that of Abraham reassures us that Lot was righteous and just but unaware of the spiritual significance of their visit.

The two angels were sent to witness how wicked Sodom was. What better way to test the inhabitants' moral standing than to assess their hospitality? Arriving in the evening, the two visitors needed food, shelter and rest, none of which they could provide for themselves. Lot offered his hospitality. At first, the visitors declined, but Lot "pressed upon them greatly," perhaps because he knew that Sodom was inhospitable to strangers, "and they turned in unto him, and entered into his house" (Gen 19:3). When they did, their welfare became his responsibility.

After his guests had feasted, "the men of the city, even the men of Sodom, compassed the house round, both old and young, all the people from every quarter" (19:4). The inclusion of everyone in the city meant that all were involved. As with one voice, "they called unto Lot, and said unto him, Where are the men which came in to thee this night? bring them out unto us, that we may know them" (19:5). One man "knowing" another was a euphemism for a homosexual act later named after the city, "sodomy." God detests sodomy as a form of sexual abuse (Lev 20:13; Rom 1:27), but their more inclusive sin appears to have been their extreme self-centeredness that gave them occasion to abuse strangers.

Because Lot's house was surrounded, the situation was inescapable. "And Lot went out at the door unto them, and shut the door after him, And said, I pray you, brethren, do not so wickedly" (Gen 19:6–7). Lot tried to calm them by begging ("I pray you") and calling them his "brethren," while at the same time he called for them to stop sinning ("do not so wickedly"). He then made a troubling offer:

> Behold now, I have two daughters which have not known man; let me, I pray you, bring them out unto you, and do ye to them as is good in your eyes: only unto these men do nothing; for therefore came they under the shadow of my roof (19:8).

Lot dealt with the situation as if he had to choose between the lesser of two evils: the rape of his daughters vs. the rape of his visitors. The truth was, rape was rape, it was against natural law, and he did not have to choose between two evils. He could have said, "over my dead body," but he was unwilling to sacrifice himself for his guests or for his daughters. By participating in the self-centered culture of Sodom, he had become too self-centered to consider that option.

As for the Sodomites, they knew that what they were doing was wicked because Lot told the entire city to "do not so wickedly." Their planned wickedness towards the visitors and Lot was willful sin, and it gave God all the evidence that He needed to destroy "all the people from every quarter" of the city and in the other cities of the plain. The crowd told Lot to "Stand back. And they said again, This one fellow came in to sojourn, and he will needs be a judge: now will we deal worse with thee, than with them. And they pressed sore upon the man, even Lot, and came near to break the door" (19:9). Lot's offer of his daughters stood, but the crowd rejected his authority to judge what was best for them, telling him that he too was a stranger in their city. They pressed ahead with their wicked plan to rape the visitors, who now included Lot.

What happened next was extraordinary. "But the men [angels] put forth their hand, and pulled Lot into the house to them, and shut the door" (19:10). Their rescue of Lot has all the markings of a rescue of the faithful from sin and death: 1) Pulling Lot into the house marked a withdrawal of his sinful offer, while it also rescued him from being crushed by the crowd at the door. The rescues were both spiritual and physical. 2) The spiritual and physical rescues occurred simultaneously, indicating that Lot was preserved because of his righteousness. If he were a straying believer, the spiritual rescue would have occurred before the physical rescue, but they occurred at the same time. 3) The physical rescue from being crushed by the crowd was accompanied by a miracle when the crowd was struck with blindness so that they could not find the door. For these reasons, we can conclude that Lot was still righteous when he was pulled in the door, despite his naturally unlawful offer.

The instructions for the escape from Sodom followed after the rapacious crowd was struck by the angels with blindness:

> And the men said unto Lot, Hast thou here any besides? son in law, and thy sons, and thy daughters, and whatsoever thou hast in the city, bring them out of this place: For we will destroy this place, because the cry of them is waxen great before the face of the Lord; and the Lord hath sent us to destroy it (Gen 19:12–13).

The angels confirmed that they were from God, and they commanded him to gather his family and "bring them out of this place." They promised him that they were going to destroy it. The command to rescue his family was also an instruction for him to escape temptation to sin ("bring them out of this place"). Had Lot obeyed the command promptly, he would have escaped further temptation, and he and his entire family would have miraculously escaped the destruction promised by the angels.

Lot at first tried to follow the command of the angels, but he failed in his mission. "And Lot went out, and spake unto his sons in law, which married his daughters, and said, Up, get you out of this place; for the Lord will destroy this city. But he seemed as one that mocked unto his sons in law" (19:14). Lot used the same words with his sons-in-law that the angels used with him. He told his sons-in-law to get "out of this place," but they thought he was joking. Lot had no more authority with his sons-in-law than he had with the people of Sodom. They disrespected him and did not follow his commands, which were from God. Since his sons-in-law were part of his family, their failure was his failure insofar as he was unable to "bring them out of this place." They chose to remain in Sodom rather than obey God. Mission failure is an unintentional form of disobedience of a command, but in Lot we see no repentance for his sin.

Instead, Lot returned home and slept spiritually as well as physically. "And when the morning arose, then the angels hastened Lot, saying, Arise, take thy wife, and thy two daughters, which are here; lest thou be consumed in the iniquity of the city" (19:15). The angels commanded him again, this time to take only his wife and daughters—the part of his family closest to him—out of Sodom. The Bible says "And while he lingered, the men laid hold upon his hand, and upon the hand of his wife, and upon the hand of his two daughters; the Lord being merciful unto him: and they brought him forth, and set him without the city" (19:16). Lot lingered and did not obey the commands of God promptly and completely.

At what point did Lot stop being an obedient believer (or righteous) and become a straying believer? With his offer of his daughters to the crowd, he was willing to break natural law, but his offer was rejected by the crowd and withdrawn by the angels. In his mission to rescue his sons-in-law, he allowed them to be disobedient, and he failed in his mission. Now ordered to take his wife and daughters out of Sodom, he lingered until the angels took them by the hand. At what point does faithfulness end and unintentional sin begin? That is one of the most important questions about Lot, and it may be unanswerable.

The evidence begins to collect, however, that Lot unintentionally became disobedient. We might find a way to excuse his failure to bring out his sons-in-law, but when he lingered in his departure from Sodom, most of us would call him unintentionally sinful, or a straying believer. "The Lord being merciful to him" implied that Lot would not receive the punishment that he now deserved.

Lot did not repent of "lingering," nor did he understand that his escape route from Sodom was also a route to redemption. "And it came to pass, when they had brought them forth abroad, that he [the angel] said, Escape for thy life; look not behind thee, neither stay thou in all the plain; escape to the mountain, lest thou be consumed" (Gen 19:17). The angels provided Lot with an escape route that would remove him from further temptation to sin (i.e., a spiritual rescue) and from the destruction of willful sinners (a physical rescue). *The* way of escape from Sodom was, unknown to Lot, a route to lead a straying believer through repentance to physical safety. Repentance would have to occur before safety because Lot was now a straying believer who had to regain the path of righteousness.

Escaping to the mountain was an opportunity to regain his righteousness, but Lot balked.

> And Lot said unto them, Oh, not so, my Lord: Behold now, thy servant hath found grace in thy sight, and thou hast magnified thy mercy, which thou hast shewed unto me in saving my life; and I cannot escape to the mountain, lest some evil take me, and I die (Gen 19:18–19).

Lot believed in God, and he was thankful to Him, but he balked at following the command to "escape to the mountain." He forsook God's mercy in providing him with *the* plan to escape sin and death.

Lot had his own escape plan in mind. "Behold now, this city is near to flee unto, and it is a little one: Oh, let me escape thither, (is it not a little one?) and my soul shall live" (19:20). The route that Lot chose only took him from a larger wicked city to a smaller wicked city named Zoar, which exists today at the foot of the Dead (or Salt) Sea. Just as choosing the lesser of two evils was sinful, so choosing the least of several wicked cities was sinful, but this time, no angel pulled Lot back from his choice. Instead of the spiritual and physical safety of the mountain, Lot went to the nearest and smallest place that would tempt him to sin.

God graciously granted his wish in order to preserve his life:

> And he [the angel] said unto him, See, I have accepted thee concerning this thing also, that I will not overthrow this city, for the which thou hast spoken. Haste thee, escape thither; for I cannot do any thing till thou be come thither (19:21-22).

God was gracious to Lot and merciful to Zoar, but Lot had unknowingly rejected the route that would have led him through repentance to a restoration of faithfulness.

Lot did not arrive in Zoar until morning of the next day, when "the Lord rained upon Sodom and upon Gomorrah brimstone and fire" (Gen 19:24). When God destroyed the city, Lot's wife looked back, violating the angel's command to "look not behind thee," and she became "a pillar of salt" (19:26). When she looked back, she suddenly became like the other Sodomites—a willful sinner—and she was punished with death.

Lot feared to remain on the plain, and he did not believe God ("I will not overthrow this city"), so he fled to the mountain where God had earlier told him to go (19:30), and he lived in a cave with his daughters. Over time, the death of his wife inspired his daughters to "make our father drink wine" (19:32) and conceive children by him, leading Lot into more unintentional sin. Through his unnatural relations with his daughters, he became the father of two tribes—Moab and Ammon—who worshipped the gods Chemosh and Milcom (Num 21:29; 1 Kgs 11:5,7).

What lessons can Christians take away from the story of Lot? First and most obviously, God condemns anyone who disobeys Him *deliberately*. The attitude of rebelliousness against God is described in the Bible as "willful" or "ungodly." We have used the term "unbeliever" to distinguish the willful sinner from the straying believer. Jesus made a similar distinction (Luke 12:47–48).

God sent His angels to Sodom to assess whether or not their sins were deliberate. The Sodomites sinned against their visitors by declaring their intent to punish them for their visit, breaking natural law. They had an opportunity to repent of their wickedness when Lot pointed out their sins and told them to stop, but they did not repent. They violated not only his command as a city judge, but a righteous command, revealing their intent to sin. After receiving confirmation of their *willful* sinning, God executed His judgment upon them, which was death. Peter said that God, "turning the cities of Sodom and Gomorrah into ashes[,] condemned them with an overthrow, making them an ensample unto those that after should live ungodly" (2 Pet 2:6). God destroyed them so that what happened would become a model ("ensample") for anyone who might choose to disobey Him deliberately. Destruction will come upon everyone who willfully sins as surely as it came upon Sodom and upon Lot's wife if they do not repent (Luke 17:28–33).

A second lesson for Christians concerns Lot and *unintentional* sin. Paul wrote to Christians in Corinth who, like Lot, were straying from obedient belief *unintentionally*. "Do not be deceived: 'Bad company corrupts good morals.' Become sober-minded as you ought, and stop sinning; for some have no knowledge of God. I speak this to your shame" (1 Cor 15:33–34 NASB). Unknowingly, many of the Christians at Corinth were in sin. As a result of their unawareness, Paul used his first letter to them to call for their repentance (2 Cor 7:8), shaming them by a letter read publicly (chastisement), but aiming at correction rather than severe punishment for all who sinned *unintentionally*.

Unintentional sin requires elevation of consciousness, either by an evangelist, by faithful members of the congregation or by the sinner him- or herself, using the Bible. All consciousness raising needs to rely on sound Christian doctrine as the basis for developing awareness of sins hidden from the immediate view of the sinner. Lot did not have a Paul to correct him, nor a congregation, nor (as do Christians today) a Bible, but the word of God has always been alive "and powerful, and sharper than any twoedged sword, piercing even to the dividing asunder of soul and spirit, and of the joints and marrow, and is a discerner of the thoughts and intents of the heart" (Heb 4:12). Lot had the words of God in the commands that the angels gave to him as part of his rescue. They tested his obedience, discerning "the thoughts and intents of the heart" which had strayed from righteousness due to self-centeredness. In Sodom, Lot had become self-centered, and his judgment had been corrupted.

The corruption of his judgment by his companionship with the Sodomites prevented Lot from following the way of escape from temptation that God provided through His angels. Instead, Lot tried to invent his own escape route (a sign of his self-centeredness), which took into account neither his lost righteousness nor his need for repentance. As a result, he repeatedly fell victim to unintentional sin. Christians need to ask themselves, "Do I resemble Lot in Sodom? Have I become self-centered rather than Christ-centered because of the culture that I am in?" Self-examination in light of what the Bible teaches about a Christ-centered life is always a productive study.

Finally, we need to take note of God's mercy with an unintentional sinner. God was patient with Lot, offering opportunities for spiritual rescue both times that angels put their hands on him. God gave him commands to follow, but neither time did Lot follow through with prompt and complete obedience to the commands. He failed to bring his whole family out. He lingered. He balked. God settled on Lot's merciful removal from Sodom so that He could destroy it. "And it came to pass, when God destroyed the cities of the plain, that God remembered [the covenant with] Abraham, and sent Lot out of the midst of the overthrow, when he overthrew the cities in the which Lot dwelt" (Gen 19:29). As in Genesis, the Hebrew for "remember" is *zakar*, which signifies acting "on a previous covenant relationship." In the end, God rescued Lot from death because Abraham was righteous, and God rewarded Abraham's righteousness with Lot's life. Lot never did repent, but neither was he rescued from unintentional sin. As a result, Lot's descendants slid into non-belief. Lot's story ends on a cautionary note, but the discovery that God tries to guide unintentional sinners like Lot should give straying believers a measure of hope.

STUDY QUESTIONS

1. Ignorance or unawareness of a sin has several causes. One is a corrupt conscience (as in the case of Lot). How

does a conscience become corrupted? How can it be restored to health?
2. Think of an example of a sin that can be willful *or* unintentional, such as someone taking something that does not belong to them, or borrowing it, but failing to return it. How does the intent of the sinner make a difference in the consequence? Give an example.
3. Unintentional sins cover more than sins of which we are unaware. They include sins that are accidental and sins that are neglectful. Think of an example of an accidental or neglectful sin. Does it still require repentance?
4. An unintentional sin can become a willful sin. What causes the change? Again, be specific. What change is there in the consequence?
5. Moses was a great leader, but he sinned when he struck a rock for water when God told him to speak to it (Num 20:11–12). What does this incident tell us about following God's commands?

6

RESCUE FROM COVETOUSNESS

Jacob

> And he [the angel] said unto him, What is thy name? And he said, Jacob. And he said, Thy name shall be called no more Jacob, but Israel: for as a prince hast thou power with God and with men, and hast prevailed (Gen 32:27–28).

Names are always significant in the Bible, and in Hebrew, *Jacob* means "Heel Grabber" or "Supplanter." The angel renamed Jacob *Israel*, or "as a prince hast thou power with God and with men, and hast prevailed" (Gen 32:28). The new name signified a change in Jacob from weakness to strength based on his experience wrestling with an angel and winning. Why did the angel—or God, for that matter—rename Jacob so that he would see himself as a powerful leader? Why was a new name appropriate? To answer these questions, we need to look into why Jacob sinned against his brother, and how God rescued him from sin.

After Rebekah, Isaac's wife, became pregnant with twins, we learn of the struggle within her over which one would be stronger than the other and born first:

> And the children struggled together within her; and she said, If it be so, why am I thus? And she went to enquire of the Lord. And the Lord said unto her, Two nations are in thy womb, and two manner of people shall be separated from thy bowels; and the one people shall be stronger than the other people; and the elder shall serve the younger (Gen 25:22–23).

If we read the prophecy carefully, we notice that it does not refer to the personal futures of the twins within Rebekah's womb. God's prophecy referred only to their descendants. The descendants would be "two nations" consisting of "two manner of people;" the "one people" stronger than "the other people;" the "elder" people serving "the younger" people. The last contrast could not refer to the twins themselves in the context of the rest of the prophecy and of history. Esau (the elder) never personally served Jacob. The misinterpretation of the prophecy to apply to the twins themselves would be important in the story.

Esau won the struggle and was born first. "And after that came his brother out, and his hand took hold on Esau's heel; and his name was called Jacob" (Gen 25:26). Esau would become the father of a nation known as Edom, and Jacob would become the father of the nation known as Israel. Esau's nation would become the elder because Esau married long before Jacob did (Gen 26:34). Over time, the stronger nation would prove to be Israel, which would subjugate Edom (Num 24:18) and fulfill the prophecy that "the elder [Edom] shall serve the younger [Israel]."

As they grew, Esau and Jacob seemed to grow apart. "And the boys grew: and Esau was a cunning hunter, a man of the field; and Jacob was a plain man, dwelling in tents" (Gen 25:27). Their contrasting lifestyles drew them apart and contributed to a growing favoritism by their parents. "Isaac loved Esau, because he did eat of his venison: but Rebekah loved Jacob" (25:28). Isaac favored Esau because of the wild game that he hunted, killed, and dressed for his father, but Rebekah favored Jacob, perhaps because of his domestic lifestyle, "dwelling in tents" near her.

By being born first, Esau received the rights of the firstborn. These rights included future leadership of the family, the judicial authority of Isaac, and a double portion of inheritance (Deut 21:17). The birthright would be exercised upon the death of his father, avoiding potential conflict among siblings for the inheritance of wealth and standing. Long before the death of Isaac, everyone in the family understood how Esau was favored by the birthright over Jacob. Furthermore, this arrangement did not conflict with the prophecy for future generations, when dominance would change so that "the elder would serve the younger" people and Israel would rule over Edom.

Despite the application of the prophecy to future nations, Jacob's desire for dominance in *his* generation became evident when Esau came to him one day while Jacob was preparing "pottage" or a meal of stew:

> And Esau came from the field, and he was faint: And Esau said to Jacob, Feed me, I pray thee, with that same red pottage; for I am faint: therefore was his name called Edom [Red]. And Jacob said, Sell me this day thy birthright. And Esau said, Behold, I am at the point to die: and what profit shall this birthright do to me? And Jacob said, Swear to me this day; and he sware unto him: and he sold his birthright unto Jacob (Gen 25:29–33).

Jacob selfishly desired Esau's birthright, which would give him dominance in the family after the death of Isaac. In exchange, Esau received a bowl of stew, which may have kept him from fainting, but which also indicated that Esau "despised his birthright" (25:34). If Jacob deserved the birthright because he wanted it more than Esau did, he also desired for himself something that rightly belonged to another person, violating God's natural law. Jacob sinned, and when he sinned, he put himself in spiritual danger.

Jacob's sin was covetousness, a great desire to possess something that belongs to someone else. Coveting his brother's birthright caused Jacob to be unjust to his brother. He strongly desired to have what by natural right did not belong to him. Later in history, God would formulate a religious command against it: "Thou shalt not covet thy neighbour's house, thou shalt not covet thy neighbour's wife, nor his manservant, nor his maidservant, nor his ox, nor his ass, nor any thing that is thy neighbour's" (Exod 20:17). The punishment for covetousness would vary depending on the value of what was coveted. For taking a neighbor's ox, the punishment was to repay him five oxen (Exod 22:1). For taking "thy neighbor's wife," the punishment was death (Lev 20:10).

Although Jacob was accountable for his covetousness, his mother Rebekah encouraged it with her own plot to steal the blessing of the firstborn for Jacob:

> And it came to pass, that when Isaac was old, and his eyes were dim, so that he could not see, he called Esau his eldest son, and said unto him, My son: and he said unto him, Behold, here am I. And he said, Behold now, I am old, I know not the day of my death: Now therefore take, I pray thee, thy weapons, thy quiver and thy bow, and go out to the field, and take me some venison; And make me savoury meat, such as I love, and bring it to me, that I may eat; that my soul may bless thee before I die. And Rebekah heard when Isaac spake to Esau his son (Gen 27: 1–5).

Rebekah's favoritism led her to promote Jacob's interests over those of Esau. When she heard Isaac's plan to bless Esau, she began to conceive a plan to trick Isaac, so that the blessing of the first born—over and above the birthright—would go to Jacob.

From her thoughts and actions, we can infer that Rebekah misinterpreted God's prophecy. She apparently believed that the elder brother, Esau, should serve the younger son, Jacob. This belief would justify her favoritism, as she sought much like Sarah (in

Chapter 4) to fulfill God's prophecy without waiting for God. If she shared her belief with Jacob, their shared belief would explain why he did not express guilt over having taken advantage of his brother. He may have believed that the prophecy justified the unequal exchange of a bowl of stew for his brother's birthright. He may have felt justified by God's prophecy instead of feeling guilty.

When Rebekah overheard Isaac tell Esau that he was about to bless him, she used what she heard to further the prospect that Jacob would dominate his brother:

> Now therefore, my son, *obey my voice* according to that which I command thee. Go now to the flock, and fetch me from thence two good kids of the goats; and I will make them savory meat for thy father, such as he loveth: And thou shalt bring it to thy father, that he may eat, and that he may bless thee before his death (Gen 27:8–10, emphasis added).

Rebekah commanded Jacob to do her will in a way that essentially supplanted God. Jacob did not want to follow her directions because he thought that his father might discover the deception and curse him rather than bless him. "And his mother said unto him, Upon me be thy curse, my son: only obey my voice, and go fetch me them" (27:13). Again, we are reminded by the phrase *obey my voice* that Rebekah attempted to supplant God with her authority, leaving Jacob to comply, which he did. His compliance in what became an elaborate scheme to deceive his nearly blind father was a sin in addition to covetousness. The only excuse for what he did was that he deceived his father at his mother's command, and that she took responsibility for the consequences.

Rebekah accurately foresaw that the blessing of the first born would further advantage Jacob. After Isaac ate the savory meat and bread that she had prepared, and after Isaac had been deceived by Jacob's disguise, Isaac said to Jacob,

God give thee of the dew of heaven, and the fatness of the earth, and plenty of corn and wine: Let people serve thee, and nations bow down to thee: be lord over thy brethren, and let thy mother's sons bow down to thee: cursed be every one that curseth thee, and blessed be he that blesseth thee (27:28–29).

Unwittingly, Isaac blessed Jacob with dominion over his brother Esau and the rest of the family. Rebekah's scheme resulted in what she mistakenly believed God had foreordained, the dominance of her favorite son.

When Esau discovered that Jacob had deceived his father, he was hurt and angry: "And he said, Is not he rightly named Jacob? For he hath supplanted me these two times: he took away my birthright; and, behold, now he hath taken away my blessing" (Gen 27:36). Esau identified Jacob's sin with his name, "Heel Grabber" or "Supplanter." Further, "Esau hated Jacob because of the blessing wherewith his father blessed him: and Esau said in his heart, The days of mourning for my father are at hand; then will I slay my brother Jacob" (27:41). What had begun for Jacob as spiritual danger now also became physical danger as Esau vowed to kill him.

Rebekah devised a way for Jacob to escape the physical threat.

> She sent and called Jacob her younger son, and said unto him, Behold, thy brother Esau, as touching thee, doth comfort himself, purposing to kill thee. Now therefore, my son, obey my voice; and arise, flee thou to Laban my brother to Haran; And tarry with him a few days, until thy brother's fury turn away (27:42–45).

As her cover story, Rebekah persuaded Isaac to send Jacob to her brother to find a wife among her nieces. Isaac commanded him to "Arise, go to Padanaram, to the house of Bethuel thy mother's father; and take thee a wife from thence of the daughters of Laban thy mother's brother" (Gen 28:2). Laban lived hundreds of miles away from Issac in Upper Mesopotamia, beyond the reach of Esau.

Although Isaac blessed Jacob's journey in the name of God, Jacob merely obeyed his father and mother when he departed. His behavior—going along with a deceitful plan, but not creating it—and his obedience to his mother in particular suggest that Jacob was a non-believer. He obeyed the commands of his father and mother, but he was not committed to obeying God. By leaving for Haran, he escaped the physical danger of being murdered, but he was in a state of sin. Furthermore, he was helplessly in this state as a non-believer. He needed a spiritual rescue, but he had not shown a belief in God. He needed to believe in God before he could be rescued from covetousness.

The story of Jacob's physical journey to Haran and back is also the story of a spiritual journey into faith. His first encounter with God was in a dream:

> and behold a ladder set up on the earth, and the top of it reached to heaven: and behold the angels of God ascending and descending on it. And, behold, the Lord stood above it, and said, I am the Lord God of Abraham thy father, and the God of Isaac: the land whereon thou liest, to thee will I give it, and to thy seed (Gen 28:12–13).

God introduced himself to Jacob, then He repeated the promise of land that He had made to his father and grandfather. He also repeated the promise to make a great people of Jacob's descendants: "And thy seed shall be as the dust of the earth, and thou shalt spread abroad to the west, and to the east, and to the north, and to the south: and in thee and in thy seed shall all the families of the earth be blessed" (28:14). God extended to Jacob the covenant first made with Abraham.

God had made his covenant with both Abraham and Isaac contingent on their obedience. Abraham was told to "Get thee out of thy country, and from thy kindred, and from thy father's house, unto a land that I will shew thee: And I will make of thee a great nation, and I will bless thee, and make thy name great; and thou shalt be a blessing" (Gen 12:1–2). The covenant required Abraham to obey God by leaving Ur for an unknown country. Isaac was required to

> Go not down into Egypt; dwell in the land which I shall tell thee of: Sojourn in this land, and I will be with thee, and will bless thee; for unto thee, and unto thy seed, I will give all these countries, and I will perform the oath which I sware unto Abraham thy father (Gen 26:2–3).

The covenant required Isaac to obey God by staying in Canaan.

No such contingency was part of the covenant with Jacob: "And, behold, I am with thee, and will keep thee in all places whither thou goest, and will bring thee again into this land; for I will not leave thee, until I have done that which I have spoken to thee of" (Gen 28:15). God made eight promises to Jacob in this dream, but He required nothing in return. He gave Jacob not a single command. Rather, God assured Jacob that He would be faithful to keep His promises.

Why? God appeared to Jacob to rescue him from his non-belief. Much like Hagar, Jacob needed to believe that God would keep His promises *before* he could follow His commands. As a non-believer, Jacob was without faith, and he needed proof that God keeps his promises in order to believe in God's word. In response to God's promises, Jacob acknowledged God's existence and presence: "Surely the Lord is in this place; and I knew it not" (28:16). By acknowledging God's presence, he surrendered his non-belief and demonstrated a belief in God, but simply believing in God did not make him an *obedient* believer.

Jacob's faith was far from mature. "And he was afraid, and said, How dreadful is this place! this is none other but the house of God [Beth-el], and this is the gate of heaven" (28:17). Jacob agreed to pursue his journey and accept God as his God, if God would fulfill His promises:

> And Jacob vowed a vow, saying, If God will be with me [future], and will keep me in this way that I go [future], and will give me bread to eat, and raiment to put on [future], So that I come again to my father's house in peace; then shall the Lord be my God [promise]: And this stone, which I have set for a pillar, shall be God's house [promise]: and of all that thou shalt give me I will surely give the tenth unto thee [promise]" (28:20–22).

Instead of God setting a contingency on His covenant, Jacob proposed his own contract with God: 'If You will protect me [future], then You shall be my God [promise].' Jacob's proposed contract with God overlooked that Jacob was the one who needed to demonstrate faithfulness, not God; nevertheless, God accepted it as a vow to Him (Gen 31:13). Jacob had yet to learn that God does not deal with people as people deal with each other.

Why did God accept Jacob's vow? One reason could be that Jacob's vow allowed God to lead Jacob more deeply into belief through God's fulfillment of His promises. Jacob was not an obedient believer, even though he had come to believe in God. "Thou believest that there is one God; thou doest well: the devils also believe, and tremble" (James 2:19). Jacob had become a straying believer, who had not yet dealt with the effect of his sins against Esau. Jacob believed in God, but he was still covetous. He may have thought that the vow to God that he had made was actually to his advantage: 'If you will provide for me and protect me, I will give you a tenth of what you give me.' Jacob may have thought that he had hired God as his scout and guide at a bargain price, but God had His own plan for Jacob, which included rescuing him from his covetousness.

While working for Laban, Jacob became the husband of four wives, the father of twelve children, "and had much cattle, and maidservants, and menservants, and camels, and asses" (Gen 30:43). How he obtained them is a story that will not be retold here. What is pertinent to Jacob's spiritual rescue was God's command to "Return unto the land of thy fathers, and to thy kindred; and I will be with thee" (Gen 31:3). To follow this command would not be easy. With his own family and herds related to Laban's family and herds, and with a brother among "thy kindred" sworn to kill him, Jacob had major physical obstacles to overcome in order to obey the command to return home.

Another obstacle was spiritual. He had grown in faith over the years as he watched God fulfill His promises to protect and prosper him. He told Leah and Rachel, "your father hath deceived me, and changed my wages ten times; but God suffered him not to hurt me" (Gen 31:7). Laban had tried to cheat Jacob repeatedly, so as a victim of Laban's covetousness, Jacob was familiar with what covetousness was. Nevertheless, he did not appear to realize that he had cheated Esau in much the same way that Laban had tried to cheat him; and that despite his believing God, he was still in sin. In short, Jacob did not realize that he was a straying believer.

Now God called for Jacob to keep his vow and obey Him. After resolving the physical obstacles to his return, Jacob journeyed with his family and their possessions towards Hebron in Canaan. To reach Canaan, the route took him to Gilead, the territory across the Jordan River from Canaan.

> And Jacob sent messengers before him to Esau his brother unto the land of Seir, the country of Edom. And he commanded them, saying, Thus shall ye speak unto my lord Esau; Thy servant Jacob saith thus, I have sojourned with Laban, and stayed there until now: And I have oxen, and asses, flocks, and menservants, and womenservants: and I have sent to tell my lord, that I may find grace in thy sight (Gen 32:3–5).

By characterizing Esau as "my lord" to his own servants, by

subordinating himself to Esau as "thy servant," and by asking for unmerited favor (grace), Jacob was not just being courteous. He was requesting a free and uncontested return home.

What frightened Jacob was the observation that his messengers brought back to him. They said that "We came to thy brother Esau, and also he cometh to meet thee, and four hundred men with him" (32:6). Jacob must have believed that Esau was still furious with him for what he had done twenty years earlier. Why else would Esau be coming so far with a force of 400 men? Jacob had only 70 people in his party, many of them women and children. He prepared to be attacked by dividing his people and herds into two camps so that one might be able to escape Esau's vengeance, then he prayed that night to God for the first time that we know of.

Jacob prayed to God for a rescue. His prayer acknowledged his humility and his willingness to obey God:

> I am not worthy of the least of all the mercies, and of all the truth, which thou has shewed unto thy servant; for with my staff I passed over this Jordan; and now I am become two bands. Deliver me, I pray thee, from the hand of my brother, from the hand of Esau: for I fear him, lest he will come and smite me, and the mother with the children. (Gen 32:10–11).

By characterizing himself as a servant of God, and by praying for a physical rescue, Jacob acknowledged that his faith in God had grown. Still, he needed God to fulfill his promise of protection (Gen 28:15). He believed that he and his family were in physical danger and helpless to escape on their own. He thought that they needed a physical rescue by God from Esau's vengeance.

The problem was that Jacob was not yet justified in God's sight. He was not an obedient believer but a straying believer, still in sin from what he had done to his brother 20 years earlier. God had a path for straying believers to become faithful, however, which was to establish their faithfulness through obedience to His commands for a spiritual rescue. Undoubtedly, that was not what Jacob had in mind, because in his prayer, he referred twice to a promise God made to him at Beth-el: "thou saidst, I will surely do thee good, and make thy seed as the sand of the sea" (Gen 32:12). A tension existed between what God would provide to straying believers, which was an opportunity for repentance, and what Jacob had expected, which was the protection promised by God until his journey ended. Which would occur first, the obedience Jacob needed or the physical rescue that he asked for? Who won this match of wills?

Jacob thought he won by the miraculous intervention of God, and God may have let him think that he won, but Jacob paid a price. Jacob did not realize what the price was, but it was repentance. His repentance began after his prayer ended: "And he lodged there that same night; and took of that which came to his hand a present for Esau his brother" (32:13). The "present" consisted of 200 she goats, 20 he goats, 200 female sheep, 20 rams, 30 milking camels with their calves, 40 cows, 10 bulls, 20 female donkeys and 10 colts. The gift was substantial, and it was to be presented herd by herd. At least five times the herdsmen would deliver the same message: These animals belong to "thy servant" Jacob, but he is giving them to "my lord Esau" as a gift. Jacob was now willing to pay Esau as compensation for his sin.

The gift was large enough that it may have made up the difference between the inheritance of Jacob and Esau. "For he said, I will appease him with the present that goeth before me, and afterward I will see his face [promise]; peradventure he will accept of me [future]" (32:20). The manner in which Jacob sought to appease Esau can be viewed as religious. As William Grasham pointed out in his commentary,[1] the Hebrew word for appeasement (*kapar*) means "cover." In a secular context, it might refer to covering himself (i.e., saving his own skin). In a spiritual context, it means "to make an atonement" or "to make a reconciliation." Today, we may be familiar with the spiritual meaning of *kapar* through Yom Kippur, or "the Day of Atonement." There is no need to abandon the spiritual meaning in favor of the secular meaning to interpret what was happening as Esau approached Jacob. If Esau was angry, Jacob estimated that his "gift" was great enough to compensate Esau for the damage done to him by Jacob's sin 20 years earlier. He could atone for his sin and cover his debt (save his own skin) at the same time.

For Jacob to repent fully, what remained was confession of his sin. To have him confess, God intervened by sending an angel as a man.

> And Jacob was left alone; and there wrestled a man with him until the breaking of the day. And when he [the angel/man] saw that he prevailed not against him, he touched the hollow of his thigh; and the hollow of Jacob's thigh was out of joint, as he wrestled with him (32:24–25).

Jacob thought that he wrestled with God and won (32:30), but later, the prophet Hosea identified the man as an angel (Hos 12:4), and Jacob won at a price, which was confession of his sin.

Esau had earlier identified Jacob's sin with his name, "Supplanter" or "Heel Grabber." "And he [the angel] said, Let me go, for the day breaketh. And he [Jacob] said, I will not let thee go, except thou bless me. And he [the angel] said unto him, What is thy name? And he said, Jacob" (Gen 32:26–27). By calling himself "Supplanter," Jacob confessed his sin. That was exactly what he needed to do to be spiritually rescued by God. In naming himself "Supplanter," he confessed his sin to the angel and to God without having to confront Esau and the possibility of vengeance.

As the spiritual rescue continued, the angel renamed Jacob and gave him a blessing. "Thy name shall be called no more Jacob, but Israel: for as a prince hast thou power with God and with men, and hast prevailed" (32:28). The angel allowed Jacob to win the wrestling match at the price of having confessed his sin. The angel then commanded that he change his name to receive the blessing of being allowed to dominate others. This command was the only command of the spiritual rescue, and we know that Jacob obeyed it because of the name he gave to the place where he built an alter to God at the end of his journey, *El-eloheIsrael* ("A Mighty God is the God of Israel").

A further price of Jacob's "victory" was the sinew or tendon in the hollow of his thigh. "Therefore the children of Israel eat not of the sinew which shrank, which is upon the hollow of the thigh, unto this day" (32:32). That shrunken tendon represented a vestige of sin. His covetousness reduced to the point of disappearing, Jacob would meet his elder brother with a gift and a limp. It was a reminder of his temptation to covet. As the patriarch of a great nation, he would be allowed to dominate others but not for the purpose of gaining what by natural right did not belong to him.

The renaming of Jacob to Israel completed Jacob's journey to obedient belief as well as his spiritual rescue. Literally translated, *Israel* meant "triumphant with God." He had been triumphant by proposing his covenant with God, which God accepted as a vow; by reminding God of His promises, which God had used to lead Jacob to obedient belief; and by repenting without having to face Esau's vengeance.

If Jacob was now faithful, and if God rescued the faithful from sin and death, we would expect a physical rescue to follow. Not surprisingly, God rescued Jacob from what appeared to Jacob to be Esau's "purposing to kill thee" (Gen 27:42). It is doubtful that Esau had travelled the long distance from Edom to Gilead with 400 men for no purpose other than to greet his brother. The two brothers met, and Jacob concluded that Esau had accepted his carefully presented atonement,

> for therefore have I seen thy face, as though I had seen the face of God, and thou wast pleased with me. Take, I pray thee, my blessing that is brought to thee; because God hath dealt graciously with me, *and because I have enough* (Gen 33:10–11, emphasis added).

Jacob considered the outcome as a miracle ("as though I had seen the face of God"). Esau was appeased, and Jacob would live.

The twins soon went their own ways. Esau went back to Mount Seir in Edom, and Jacob went to the town of Succoth in Canaan, then to a village near Shechem, where he built the altar to God. He would never be covetous again, but he would walk with a limp the rest of his life, "leaning on the top of his staff" (Heb 11:21).

The end of the story reminds us that when a straying believer confronts their own sin, names it, and further repents of it, God releases them from condemnation (a spiritual rescue), accepts them as an obedient believer and grants them life (a physical rescue). What made Jacob's situation special was that after his initial belief in God, he carried his sin with him 20 more years before he repented and became an obedient believer.

Jacob's situation may have been special, but it is far from unique. Anyone who as an adult has confronted and repented of a sin deeply embedded in their character knows that they have been in sin a long time, and that they cannot walk away from the sin without a limp—a reminder of their long-standing temptation to sin. Christians' imperfections as human beings allow them to walk forward spiritually in no other way. Just because repentant sinners have been forgiven does not put them out of the reach of temptation. To walk on this earth without sin is *not* to walk without temptation. Just the opposite. To walk without sin is to walk with awareness of temptation and to continue to resist it.

Jesus used a different metaphor to communicate the same idea. He said, "If any man will come after me, let him deny himself, and take up his cross daily, and follow me" (Luke 9:23). As Christians dedicate themselves to doing God's will, the cross that they pick up is their enduring temptation to sin: To go their own way rather than the Way of Jesus Christ. The burden of the cross is a reminder that even though Christians may not run as they did before they confronted their characteristic sins, they can walk on this earth without sin, if they walk carefully and if they follow Him.

STUDY QUESTIONS

1. One dictionary defines covetousness as "immoderate desire for the possession of something, especially wealth." Show how this definition applied to Jacob before he left Canaan, and explain why it did not apply to him as he returned.
2. Covetousness frequently leads to other sins. Name another sin that might have covetousness as its root and foundation.
3. Jacob's promise to God (Gen 28:20–21) was different than God's promise to Jacob (Gen 31:3). What made Jacob's travel to Padanaram and back a journey into faith?
4. Jacob believed in God many years before believing God, or repenting of sin and consciously trying to do His will. Do you think this situation was common during Christ's ministry? Why? Do you think it is common today?
5. Have you privately identified a weakness that repeatedly leads you to be tempted to sin? Have you ever had to confess and repent of this characteristic sin? What did repentance involve?

7

RESCUE FROM IDOLATRY REFUSED

Exodus

> Then said I unto them, Cast ye away every man the abominations of his eyes, and defile not yourselves with the idols of Egypt: I am the Lord your God. But they rebelled against me, and would not hearken unto me (Ezek 20:7–8).

Exodus is often told as the story of a rescue of the Israelites from Egyptian oppression, but another way to think of it is as an opportunity for the Israelites to escape Egyptian idolatry. One commentary has noted, "The call of God by Moses was as much to them to separate from idols and follow Jehovah, as it was to Pharaoh to let them go forth."[1] Viewing the exodus in terms of Israelite idolatry is different from the usual focus on Pharaoh and the escape from physical oppression. It relies more on Ezekiel's account of what happened than that of Moses, and more on the brief accounts in the New Testament than those in the Old Testament.

To explore the exodus in this light, we need to consider first, Moses' account of the exodus; second, Ezekiel's account; and third, the New Testament view, as briefly presented in several passages.

The principle of complimentarity should allow us then to see an overview of the exodus and teach us its value for Christians today.

MOSES' ACCOUNT OF THE EXODUS

In Chapter 6, we learned that Jacob, his family and his household (the Israelites) entered Canaan. Some years later, his next to youngest son, Joseph, who was his favorite son, was sold into slavery by his envious brothers, who told their father that Joseph had been killed. Joseph entered Egypt as a slave, but due to the grace of God and the talents that God gave to him, he was freed from slavery and became second in rank only to Pharaoh, the king of Egypt. During a famine in Canaan, Jacob sent Joseph's brothers to Egypt for food. Joseph was reconciled with his family, which moved to Egypt.

Pharaoh settled the family in Goshen, a fertile land on the eastern side of the Nile River. Jacob and his 13 children died there, his grandchildren prospered, and over the next 430 years, the Israelites grew into a nation of 600,000 men (Num 11:21) plus women and children, called "the children of Israel," or simply, "Israel." We know that Jacob worshipped God. The question is, did his extended family believe in God 430 years later?

Conditions changed over that length of time. Pharaohs had come and gone, and the Israelites lost favor in their sight. The last pharaoh to rule over them had enslaved them to use as labor to build two "treasure" cities. He considered their large number and location on Egypt's eastern border a threat because they might join forces with his enemies to the east. For the security of his own people, he planned to absorb the Israelites slowly into the Egyptian population by killing the male babies as they were born, but the Israelite midwives would not cooperate. He then ordered his people to slay the male infants by throwing them in the River, but one who escaped was found by Pharaoh's daughter to be floating in a basket. She adopted him as her son, and unknowingly, chose his birth mother as his wet nurse. Pharaoh's daughter named him "Moses." He was raised as a member of the royal family, but his mother, who remained with him, undoubtedly taught him who he really was, an Israelite.

As the Hebrew writer reminds us, Moses was led by faith in God from the time he became a man. "By faith Moses, when he was come to years, refused to be called the son of Pharaoh's daughter; choosing rather to suffer affliction with the people of God, than to enjoy the pleasures of sin for a season" (Heb 11:24–25). Moses' faith in God led him to identify with the Israelites rather than with the Egyptians. After he killed an Egyptian who was punishing an Israelite, he fled to the land of Midian. "By faith he forsook Egypt, not fearing the wrath of the king: for he endured, as seeing him who is invisible" (11:27). His faith in God was the motive for his actions (Acts 7:24–25), and it justified him in the sight of God. Moses was an obedient believer.

One day while Moses was shepherding, God attracted his attention by setting a bush on fire, but it continued to burn without burning up. Out of curiosity, Moses approached the burning bush, God called his name, and He commanded Moses to "put off thy shoes from off thy feet, for the place whereon thou standest is holy ground" (Exod 3:5). The "place" was Mount Sinai—also called Mount Horeb—and by taking off his shoes, Moses obeyed God, evidence of his obedient belief. God chose Moses to lead the Israelites out of Egypt and into Canaan, the land that He had promised to the children of Israel.

Moses did not think that the Israelites would believe that he had met with God. "And Moses said unto God, Behold, when I come unto the children of Israel, and shall say unto them, The God of your fathers hath sent me unto you; and they shall say to me, What is his name? what shall I say unto them?" (3:13). God replied, "I AM THAT I AM: and he said, Thus shalt thou say unto the children of Israel, I AM hath sent me unto you" (3:14). Whatever else

God meant, He commanded Moses to declare his existence to the Israelite people.

What could have made the name "I AM" more appropriate to the Israelite people than one of His other names (e.g., Jehovah or Lord)? One possibility is that after 430 years in Egypt, many of the Israelites no longer believed that He existed. They were aware of God's past existence through stories about their dead ancestors, but many of them had never believed in Him themselves. Recall that a non-believer, as defined in Chapter 1, might worship other gods. The Egyptians, who worshipped other gods, were non-believers.

God tested Moses' belief in Him. He commanded Moses to throw to the ground the shepherd's rod that he had in his hand. It became a snake, "and Moses fled from before it" (Exod 4:3), presumably out of fear of snakes. To measure his belief, "the Lord said unto Moses, Put forth thine hand, and take it by the tail. And he put forth his hand, and caught it, and it became a rod in his hand" (4:4). For a man afraid of snakes, following this command from God tested his obedience. The miracle of turning the rod into a snake and then back again, which was later demonstrated in front of the Israelites, then again in front of Pharaoh, was first used privately by God with Moses. It tested Moses' faith, and he passed the test.

God gave Moses and later his brother, Aaron, the power to work this miracle so that the Israelites "may believe that the Lord God of their fathers, the God of Abraham, the God of Isaac, and the God of Jacob, hath appeared unto thee" (4:5). If this miracle did not create belief, God gave Moses the power to work two other miracles for the same purpose.

> Put now thine hand into thine bosom. And he put his hand into his bosom: and when he took it out, behold, his hand was leprous as snow. And he said, Put thine hand into thine bosom again. And he put his hand into his bosom again; and plucked it out of his bosom, and behold, it was turned again as his other flesh (4:6–7).

Suddenly to become leprous was as much a miracle as its cure. "If they will not believe also these two signs, neither hearken unto thy voice, that thou shalt take of the water of the river, and pour it upon the dry land: and the water which thou takes out of the river shall become blood upon the dry land" (4:9). Three three miracles were provided to Moses and Aaron that the people might believe them and believe God.

The display of "signs" or miracles took place in front of the elders of the Israelites. "And Moses and Aaron went and gathered together all the elders of the children of Israel: And Aaron spake all the words which the Lord had spoken unto Moses, and did the signs in the sight of the people" (4:29–30). Aaron performed all three miracles before convincing the elders of what they had been told: The God of their ancestors not only continued to exist, but He had come to lead them out of Egypt and into a land flowing with milk and honey. "And the people believed: and when they heard that the Lord had visited the children of Israel, and that he had looked upon their affliction, then they bowed their heads and worshipped" (4:31). Sharing with them God's message and working the signs in the sight of the people inspired the Israelites to believe in God, but we have to look beyond the account in the Book of Exodus to find the rest of the story.

EZEKIEL'S ACCOUNT OF THE EXODUS

More than 850 years later, rebellious Israelite leaders visited the prophet Ezekiel to "inquire of the Lord" (Ezek 20:1). The response was, "As I live, saith the Lord God, I will not be inquired of by you" (20:3) because of their willful sins. Rather, He told Ezekiel to "cause them to know the abominations of their fathers" (20:4), beginning with their idolatry in Egypt:

> In the day that I lifted up mine hand unto them, to bring them forth of the land of Egypt into a land that I had espied for them,

flowing with milk and honey, which is the glory of all lands: Then said I unto them, Cast ye away every man the abominations of his eyes, and defile not yourselves with the idols of Egypt: I am the Lord your God. But they rebelled against me, and would not hearken unto me: they did not every man cast away the abominations of their eyes, neither did they forsake the idols of Egypt: then I said, I will pour out my fury upon them, to accomplish my anger against them in the midst of the land of Egypt. (Ezek 20:6–8)

The phrase *lifted my hand* meant "promised," just as today, someone might lift up their hand to promise to tell the truth. God through Ezekiel spoke about a promise made on a given day. That promise was "I will bring you up out of the affliction of Egypt unto the the land of the Canaanites" (Exod 3:17). The day that Aaron "spake all the words [including this promise] which the Lord had spoken unto Moses" (Exod 4:30) to the elders of Israel was *the same day* that the Lord told the Israelites to throw away their idols and stop worshipping them.

Today, someone casually reading the book of Exodus, written under divine inspiration by Moses, would not realize that the day that "the people believed" was the very same day that "they rebelled against me, and would not hearken unto me" (Ezek 20:8). The reader would have to see how the account of Ezekiel, also written under divine inspiration, compliments the account of Moses. When the Israelites believed in God, they would not throw away the idols that they had been worshipping in Egypt. They just added God to the Egyptian gods that they worshipped, missing only a physical representation (idol) for Him. The Israelites were what are called "polytheists," people who believe in or worship more than one god.

What caused the Israelites to "rebel," or to become intentionally sinful, was their violation of commands from God. "Cast ye away" and "defile not" are verbs in the imperative mood. God commanded the Israelites to 1) throw away their idols and 2) stop worshipping them on the same day that they began to worship Him. These commands pre-existed the Ten Commandments. They confirm that the Israelites were worshipping idols that represented the gods of Egypt *before* they became believers in Jehovah God, and they refused to stop, even as they began worshipping God. They never were obedient believers, nor were they ever straying believers —believers who were in unintentional sin. They were *unbelievers* from the moment that "the people believed."

In Chapter 1, an *unbeliever* was defined as a person who consciously rejects belief in the one true God and His word. Did the Israelites consciously do that? Through Ezekiel, God said that they "rebelled" and "would not hearken," both of which indicate a willful rejection of God's word. Further, they did not accept that only one God existed. In other words, by keeping their idols, they consciously rejected belief in the one true God *and* His word. They were not only examples of unbelievers (like the people of the ancient world, or the residents of Sodom). They were models of unbelief, defying God at every turn of events.

God wanted to destroy them in Egypt because of their willful disobedience,

> But I wrought for my name's sake, that it should not be polluted before the heathen, among whom they were, in whose sight I made myself known unto them, in bringing them forth out of the land of Egypt. Wherefore I caused them to go forth out of the land of Egypt, and brought them into the wilderness (Ezek 20:9–10).

In front of Egyptians as well as the Israelites, God had promised to bring the Israelites out of Egypt, but if He had destroyed the Israelites in Egypt for their unbelief, He would not have been able to keep His promise to bring them out. God "wrought" or worked the miracles of the exodus for His reputation. He was faithful to keep His promises, even if the Israelites willfully disobeyed Him.

From the Exodus story by Moses, we are familiar with what these miracles were. They included the ten plagues to persuade Pharaoh to let the Israelites go into the desert, the parting of the Red Sea, the destruction of the pursuing Egyptian army, the daily provision of "manna" for food and the creation of drinkable water at Massah and Meribah. According to God's word spoken by Ezekiel, all of these miracles were designed to allow the Israelites to be removed from Egypt into the wilderness or desert, where God gave them what is sometimes called "the law of Moses:"

> And I gave them my statutes, and shewed them my judgments, which if a man do, he shall even live in them. Moreover also I gave them my sabbaths, to be a sign between me and them, that they might know that I am the Lord that sanctify them. But the house of Israel rebelled against me in the wilderness: they walked not in my statutes, and they despised my judgments, which if a man do, he shall even live in them; and my sabbaths they greatly polluted: then I said, I would pour out my fury upon them in the wilderness to consume them (Ezek 20:11–13).

Moses recorded the statutes and judgments (a sort of common law), which would have led the Israelites to live, if they had obeyed them, but they rebelled, and the implication was that they would die because of the nature of their disobedience, which was willful or intentional sin. As unbelievers, they consciously rejected God's statutes and judgments, even though these laws represented the word of God.

The only reason that God did not kill the Israelites in the desert before they arrived at Canaan was His reputation for faithfulness to His promises. "But I wrought for my name's sake, that it should not be polluted before the heathen, in whose sight I brought them out" (Ezek 20:14). God protected his reputation by keeping most of the Israelites alive. His reputation would prove to be invaluable for the conquest of Canaan because it would weaken the resistance of the people who lived there to the Israelite invasion.

Once the Israelites reached Canaan, Moses sent twelve spies into Canaan to scout the land, but ten of them returned with an "evil" or unfavorable report (Num 13:32). The people believed the unfavorable report and decided not to enter Canaan, rejecting God's promise of a homeland.

> Yet also I lifted up my hand unto them in the wilderness, that I would not bring them into the land which I had given them, flowing with milk and honey, which is the glory of all lands; Because they despised my judgments, and walked not in my statutes, but polluted my sabbaths: for their heart went after their idols (Ezek 20:15–16).

Ezekiel reminded his listeners that Israelite idolatry was the source of their unbelief in the fulfillment of His promise ("the land which I had given to them"). He promised now that He would not bring them into the land.

In the end, "mine eye spared them from destroying them, neither did I make an end of them in the wilderness" (20:17). God did not completely destroy them in the desert because He preserved the next generation—those under 20 when they left Egypt—and covenanted with them. The possibility exists that the Ten Commandments, as well as other statutes and judgments, were given to the Israelites primarily for the benefit of their descendants. Speaking to the next generation not long before he died, Moses said, "The Lord made not this covenant with our fathers, but with us, even us, who are all of us here alive this day" (Deut 5:3). Except for Joshua and Calleb, Moses' audience consisted only of the next generation. Everyone else had either been killed because of their unbelief or died off. Their deaths were spread over 40 years and hundreds of miles, so God's reputation for keeping His promises was preserved.

The covenant with future generations may be why the Ten Commandments were written in stone, so that the most important laws could be passed down unchanged for generations to come. The older generation was lost in unbelief through their refusal to throw away their idols and stop worshiping them. It had refused the opportunity of a rescue from sin by refusing to obey two simple commands, "Cast ye away every man the abominations of his eyes, and defile not yourselves with the idols of Egypt" (Ezek 20:7). These commands were sequenced to make them easier to follow. If the Israelites had thrown their idols away, nothing would have remained for them to worship except God. Ceasing worship of idols was easier without the idols around than if they had been present.

Further, the first two of the Ten Commandments were a version of the instructions that God gave to the Israelites in Egypt. If they had only followed them, they would have been rescued from the sin of idolatry:

> I am the Lord thy God, which have brought thee out of the land of Egypt, out of the house of bondage. Thou shalt have no other gods before me. Thou shalt not make unto thee any graven image, or any likeness of any thing that is in heaven above, or that is in the earth beneath, or that is in the water under the earth: Thou shalt not bow down thyself to them, nor serve them: for I the Lord thy God am a jealous God (Exod 20:2–5).

No other gods "before me" (*al panai* in Hebrew) literally meant "before My face." The first two great commands of the Ten were nearly identical in meaning to the two commandments given to the Israelites while in Egypt—to throw away their idols (no other gods "before My face," no manufacture of idols), and to stop worshipping them (no bowing to them nor serving them). The significant difference between the earlier commandments and the first two of the Ten Commandments was in the amount of detail. God meant for the people to destroy their idols, and *never replace them;* to stop worshipping them, and *never show them any respect.* The first two of the Ten Commandments were clarifications of the commands given in Egypt for the rescue of the Israelites from the sin of idolatry. They were put first not so much as a reminder to the unbelieving generation of their idolatry, as they were a perpetual offer to future generations of a rescue from idolatry, if they would obey these two commands: Throw away your idols, and stop worshipping them.

ACCOUNTS IN THE NEW TESTAMENT

What can the Christian learn from the Israelite refusal of a rescue from the sin of idolatry? Paul began to answer this question when he said,

> Brethren, I would not that ye should be ignorant, how that all our fathers were under the cloud, and all passed through the sea; and were all baptized unto Moses in the cloud and in the sea; And did all eat the same spiritual meat; and did all drink the same spiritual drink; for they drank of that spiritual Rock that followed them: and that Rock was Christ (1 Cor 10:1–4).

Paul considered that the Israelites in the exodus were a foreshadow of Christians, having been "baptized unto Moses" instead of into Christ, with "spiritual meat" and "spiritual drink" or what corresponds to the body and blood of Christ (the Lord's supper) to sustain them spiritually and physically. Their spiritual and physical experiences in the exodus were a model, not in the sense that they represented an ideal but in the sense that they were a prefiguration. Paul realized that what happened to the Israelites could happen to the Christians.

Consequently, Paul warned the Corinthians. "But with many of them God was not well pleased: for they were overthrown in the wilderness" (10:5). The Greek word for "overthrown" here comes from the noun, *katastrophe*, which is an easily recognizable root for English speakers. The catastrophe that happened to the Israelites could happen to the Christians. "Now these things were our examples, to the intent we should not lust after evil things, as they also lusted" (10:6). Many things were evil because they were forbidden by God, but the first was idolatry. "Neither be ye idolaters, as were some of them; as it is written, The people sat down to eat and drink, and rose up to play" (10:7). Paul referred specifically to Moses' account of the creation of the golden calf while he was receiving the Ten Commandments at Mount Sinai (Exod 32:1–6). "Play" refers to the joking, singing, and dancing that surrounded idol worship. Punishment for worshipping the golden calf involved breaking the tablets of the Ten Commandments, burning and grinding the idol into powder to be drunk by the worshippers, and the execution of 3,000 worshippers. In the next verse, Paul referred to an incident before the entrance into Canaan involving illicit relations with Moabite women encouraged by worship of a Canaanite god (Num 25:1–9). "Neither let us commit fornication, as some of them committed, and fell in one day, three and twenty thousand" (1 Cor 10:8).

The next two examples of sins to be avoided were the indirect results of idol worship because they stemmed from unbelief, or the rejection of God and His word. "Neither let us tempt Christ, as some of them also tempted, and were destroyed of serpents" (10:9). This incident of testing God involved the desire of the Israelites for something better to eat than manna, the bread that God had given to them to sustain them in their wandering. "And the Lord sent fiery serpents among the people, and they bit the people; and much people of Israel died" (Num 21:6). Their deaths prefigured the deaths of any Christian who would test Christ. "Neither murmur ye, as some of them also murmured, and were destroyed of the destroyer" (1 Cor 10:10). God summarized the rebellious murmurings of the Israelites: "How long shall I bear with this evil congregation, which murmur against me? I have heard the murmurings of the children of Israel, which they murmur against me" (Num 14:27). The punishment would be that generation would never enter Canaan. "Doubtless ye shall not come into the land, concerning which I sware to make you dwell therein, save Caleb the son of Jephunneh, and Joshua the son of Nun" (14:30). The warning to Christians was clear. If they committed idolatry, or any of the sins associated with it either directly or indirectly, they would not enter heaven.

That warning sounds harsh to our ears, but Paul was not writing about unintentional sins that might be committed from ignorance, neglect, or accident. He was writing about intentional sins, or sins committed by someone who has the knowledge not to commit them. The Israelites had known ever since they became believers: Throw away your idols and stop worshipping them. They even carried those commandments in stone. Nevertheless, they broke them willfully, as if they had never existed.

Paul began his warning, "Brethren, I would not that ye should be ignorant." He wanted them to know about the sins of the Israelites, but knowledge of sin carried a risk of even greater sin—intentional sin. That was the greater danger because punishment for it could become inescapable, as shown by the experience of the exodus. That was also the most important lesson of the exodus for Christians. Punishment could become inescapable for the willful sinner, and that punishment included death without the possibility of heaven (spiritual Canaan). "Now all these things happened unto them for ensamples [models]: and they are written for our admonition, upon whom the ends of the world are come" (1 Cor 10:11). Paul was not simply warning Christians that they should not sin. He was warning them that they should not sin like the Israelites in the exodus from Egypt ("ensamples"), that is, willfully, in the knowledge that they were sinning. The danger was not that Christians in Corinth were being deceived by someone or something, but that they were deceiving themselves in thinking that they were without sin. So too today, "If we say that we have no sin, we deceive ourselves, and the truth is not in us. If we confess our sins, he is faithful and just to forgive us our sins, and to cleanse us from all unrighteousness (1 John 1:8–9).

Consequently, Paul warned them, "Wherefore let him that thinketh he standeth take heed lest he fall" (1 Cor 10:12). There were some Corinthians (like Caleb and Joshua in the exodus) who were without sin, but there were others who were in sin and had done nothing about their condition. They had all been baptized, and they were all partakers of the body and blood of Jesus Christ, but there were some who had awareness of sin and who had not repented. Paul appealed to these Christians, who like the Israelites, were in unbelief:

> There hath no temptation taken you but such as is common to man: but God is faithful, who will not suffer you to be tempted above that ye are able; but with the temptation also make a ["the" NASB] way of escape, that ye may be able to bear it. Wherefore, my dearly beloved, flee from idolatry (10:13–14).

Paul concluded that the root sin in Corinth, as in Egypt, was idolatry. From it had flowed other sins, including intentional sin, but Paul reminded them that God also created the way to escape even their willful sin. The Israelites carried the means to escape temptation everywhere they went, written in stone, in the Ark of the Covenant (Heb 9:4): The commands written on them were destroy your idols, and *never replace* them, stop worshipping them, and *never show them any respect*. Or in Paul's brief command, "Flee from idolatry."

Jesus realized that idols were not always stone statues or engravings. "No man can serve two masters: for either he will hate the one, and love the other; or else he will hold to the one, and despise the other. Ye cannot serve God and mammon (Matt 6:24). *Mammon* does not refer to a mythical god, but it is a transliteration of an Aramaic word for "riches.' Jesus understood that "masters" do not have to be gods in a traditional sense, but they are any thing or any one that is most important in life. Service to God and His Son must *always* be first for a Christian to be faithful.

The other information about the exodus in the New Testament is found in Hebrews, Chapter 3. The advice that the Hebrew writer gave to Hebrew Christians has less to do with idolatry as a source of sin than with self-deception as a result of sin. Although idolatry had been a problem among Hebrews in the past, it was largely confined to the Gentiles in Paul's day. The Hebrew writer told Christians (most of whom were Hebrews) to "Harden not your hearts, as in the provocation, in the day of temptation in the wilderness: When your fathers tempted me, proved me, and saw my works forty years" (Heb 3:8–9). The Hebrew writer quoted Psalm 95. Why? He warned the Hebrew Christians not so much of the origins of unbelief as he warned them of its consequences. "Wherefore I was grieved with that generation, and said, They do alway err in their heart; and they have not known my ways. So I share in my wrath, They shall not enter into my rest" (Heb 3:10–11). The Hebrew writer was warning Christians not to sin willfully. Drifting or straying from God was one thing. Departing from God was another. "Take heed, brethren, lest there be in any of you an evil heart of unbelief, in departing from the living God" (3:12). Willful departure of the Hebrew Christians from "the living God" would be punished as it was punished in the days of the exodus. If the heart were hardened to the point of unbelief, going to heaven would be impossible. Consequently, Christians needed to "exhort one another daily" to strengthen each other in their hope of salvation. "For we are made partakers of Christ, if we hold the beginning of our confidence steadfast unto the end" (Heb 3:14). Heaven would become their homeland, as partners with Christ, if they maintained their faith ("our confidence") in Him as they had at the beginning, "until the end."

What might "the end" be? It might be the end of the world, at which time the faithful in Jesus Christ will be rewarded with life in heaven. This reward is a far better and more joyful reward than a blessed life on earth, which as far as our case studies have found, was all that God offered to people as a reward for their righteousness under the old covenant. How much better the new covenant is, which offers both rescues in life and at the end of life for those who are faithful "until the end."

Study Questions

1. An idol is "an image or representation of a god used as an object of worship" (*OED*). Except in books for little children (who need pictures to understand), "life-like" representations of Jesus Christ and God are missing in church buildings. Why?
2. Joshua and Caleb were the only Israelites of their generation to cross over the border to possess Canaan. Everyone else died in the desert. What made Joshua and Caleb different from the other Israelites? Cite specific passages.
3. "Apostasy" is popularly considered an unusual situation in which someone says "I don't believe in God anymore." How does apostasy (unbelief) often begin much earlier than that?
4. The Israelites of the exodus were spiritually insensitive (Exod 32:9, 33:3). The hymn "Amazing Grace" includes the lyric, "I once was lost, but now am found, was blind but now I see." What is now seen?
5. How does Psalm 37:25 give Christians hope in life? In relation to Matthew 6:33, what kinds of risks does it encourage Christians to take?

8

RESCUE FROM A SINFUL PAST

Rahab

And Joshua saved Rahab the harlot alive, and her father's household, and all that she had; and she dwelleth in Israel even unto this day; because she hid the messengers, which Joshua sent to spy out Jericho (Josh 6:25).

After their first attempt to enter Canaan failed, the Israelites wandered 38 years in the desert until the generation that had left Egypt as adults (with the exceptions of Joshua and Caleb) died in the desert as punishment for their rebelliousness. Their children, grown to adulthood and newly pledged to obey Joshua (Josh 1:16), finally camped at Abel-Shittim, just across the Jordan River from Canaan (see map). Joshua sent two men from camp "to spy secretly, saying, Go view the land, even Jericho. And they went, and came into an harlot's house, named Rahab, and lodged there" (Josh 2:1). Jericho was a walled Canaanite city across the River from the Israelites. From these few words about Rahab, we know that she was a Canaanite, a householder, and a prostitute who made her living in a sinful city. She probably owned a brothel that served as an inn. She was not a virtuous woman—just the opposite

—so why would God rescue her from sin? The short answer is that she hid the Israelite spies, but there is much more to her remarkable story.

By the standards of God's laws, Canaan was a land filled with sinful religious and social practices. Passages in Leviticus reveal how sinful the practices of the Canaanites were. God commanded the Israelites:

- "After the doings of the land of Egypt, wherein ye dwelt,

shall ye not do: and after the doings of the land of Canaan, whither I bring you, shall ye not do" (Lev 18:3)
- "Defile not ye yourselves in any of these things: for in all these the nations are defiled which I cast out before you: And the land is defiled: therefore I do visit the iniquity thereof upon it, and the land itself vomiteth out her inhabitants." (Lev 18:24–25)
- "For whosoever shall commit any of these abominations, even the souls that commit them shall be cut off from among their people." (Lev 18:29)

"The doings," "these things" and "these abominations" were an assortment of Canaanite customs: Incest (18:6–18), adultery (18:20), human sacrifice (18:21), profane use of the name of the Lord (18:21), homosexuality (18:22) and bestiality (18:23). As a result of these customary practices, "the land is defiled" (18:25), and the "nations" or tribes that defiled it were to be driven out of the land or destroyed, along with any Israelites who joined in their sins.

On their journey towards Canaan, the Israelites had to pass by a city called Heshbon (ruled by King Sihon) and a kingdom called Bashan (ruled by King Og). God told Joshua, "behold, I have given into thine hand Sihon the Amorite, king of Heshbon, and his land: begin to possess it, and contend with him in battle" (Deut 2:24). At first, the Israelites attempted to pass by Heshbon peacefully, "But Sihon king of Heshbon would not let us pass by him: for the Lord thy God hardened his spirit, and made his heart obstinate, that he might deliver him into thy hand, as appeareth this day" (2:30). The result was a slaughter. The Israelites "utterly destroyed the men, and the women, and the little ones, of every [part of the] city, we left none to remain" (2:34). When they came to Bashan, similar events occurred near Edrei, "So the Lord our God delivered into our hands Og also, the king of Bashan, and all his people: and we smote him until none was left to him remaining" (Deut 3:3). One of the effects of these battles was the uncontested encampment of the

Israelites at Abel-Shittim. Another was the terrifying reputation of the Israelites and their God.

God's reputation and that of the Israelites made the conquest of Canaan easier. When they began their journey through Heshbon and Bashan, God told them, "This day will I begin to put the dread of thee and the fear of thee upon the nations that are under the whole heaven, who shall hear report of thee, and shall tremble, and be in anguish because of thee" (Deut. 2:25). It is reasonable to assume that Rahab's inn would have been alive with talk of the utter destruction of the two cities across the River. Talk would have been motivated by fear of what the Israelites and their God would do next.

Three days before the Israelites were to cross the Jordan River, Joshua sent two of his men across the Jordan River to Jericho "to spy secretly" (Josh 2:1), but the king of Jericho was told about the spies the same evening that they entered his city. "And it was told the king of Jericho, saying, Behold, there came men in hither to night of the children of Israel to search out the country" (2:2). The king knew that the spies were Israelites, that they were in the city, what their mission was, and even where they were staying. "And the king of Jericho sent unto Rahab, saying, Bring forth the men that are come to thee, which are entered into thine house: for they be come to search out all the country" (2:3). The spies had not entered the city secretly, and their mission to "go view the land, even Jericho" (2:1) was in jeopardy from the start.

The mission of the spies had somehow become known through the spies. The spies were in danger of being captured and killed. The danger was physical, but their capture would become a spiritual matter if it ended their mission. The spies had obeyed a command from Joshua to go on a mission. Joshua's authority came from God. Joshua's commands were treated as Moses' commands: "According as we hearkened unto Moses in all things, so will we hearken unto thee" (Josh 1:17). Failing to accomplish the mission by ignorance, accident, or neglect would be a sin because the mission was commanded, and failing to execute the command—even unintentionally—would be a failure to keep the commandment.

The mission had not yet failed because the spies had not yet been captured. While the servants sent by the king waited outside for Rahab, she "took the two men, and hid them" (Josh 2:4), then she reported to the king:

> There came men unto me, but I wist not whence they were: And it came to pass about the time of shutting of the gate, when it was dark, that the men went out: whither the men went I wot not: pursue after them quickly; for ye shall overtake them (2:4–5).

Rahab invented a story that she knew was a lie in order to cover up the presence of the spies and their location. She hid the men on her roof among stalks of flax that were drying (2:6) should the king not believe her and search her house.

The king believed her story, but he also unwittingly trapped the spies in Jericho when he shut the gate. "And the men pursued after them the way to Jordan unto the fords: and as soon as they which pursued after them were gone out, they shut the gate" (2:7). The king not only assumed that the spies had left the city, as Rahab had falsely reported to him, but he sent men to capture them along the road to the Jordan River. When the king shut the gate as a precaution from the attack that he now expected, no one could enter the city, but no one could leave. Whether or not the Canaanites discovered them, the spies were now helpless to obey the command to "go view the land, even Jericho." Buried under flax, they could not even view the city from Rahab's rooftop. They needed both a spiritual rescue to complete their mission and a physical rescue to escape alive from a wicked city.

Before the spies lay down to sleep, "she came up unto them upon the roof; And she said unto the men, I know that the Lord hath given you the land, and that your terror is fallen upon us, and that all the inhabitants of the land faint because of you" (Josh 2:8–

9). It is likely that Rahab believed that God had given Canaan to the Israelites as part of what she had heard about them:

> For we have heard how the Lord dried up the water of the Red Sea for you, when ye came out of Egypt; and what ye did unto the two kings of the Amorites, that were on the other side Jordan, Sihon and Og, whom ye utterly destroyed (2:10).

Rahab was well-informed about God and the Israelites, and she believed what she heard.

While other Canaanites were discouraged by what they heard, Rahab believed it. That is why she told the spies that she *knew* "the Lord hath given you the land." She could not have said that had she not believed enough of what she heard to conclude that the Israelites would conquer Canaan, including Jericho. Her complete belief was confessed to the spies: "And as soon as we had heard these things, our hearts did melt, neither did there remain any more courage in any man, because of you: for the Lord your God, he is God in heaven above, and in earth beneath" (2:11). Rahab's confession of belief in God as the one God ("in heaven above, and in earth beneath") represented her conversion from a non-believer to an obedient believer. She confessed her belief before two witnesses, who apparently were required to establish a fact legally (Deut 19:15).

Her confessed belief in God put her in jeopardy because it obliged her to be faithful to God and His commands rather than to the king and his commands, if the two conflicted. She could not live as she had lived in the past. Lying and her livelihood had to change. She was in danger not only from the king, who might discover that she had lied to protect the enemy, but also from the Israelites who might slay her and her family in the complete and utter destruction of Jericho. Even though she had a means of escaping the city by a rope through a window in the wall (Josh 2:15), she was helpless to escape a dilemma: Execution by the Canaanites as a traitor, if they discovered that she hid the spies; or destruction by the forces of God, within or without the city, if the Canaanites did not discover her first. Her predicament was generally similar to that of the spies. They were all obedient believers who needed both a spiritual rescue and a physical rescue.

We learned from the case of Noah that such rescues occur simultaneously because the ones being rescued are already obedient believers. Their rescue does not remove sin from them, but it removes them from sin. With its gate shut, the city of Jericho was like the ancient world in Noah's day. Every adult, every child, every animal left in the city was to be destroyed—no one and nothing was to be left alive. The cultures in Canaan had become so unnatural and the land had become so defiled that it needed to be cleansed, just as the earth needed cleansing at the time of Noah. The destruction of Jericho meant the destruction of the evil that appeared to surround Rahab and the spies. Consequently, the rescue of them physically (to save their lives) also meant the rescue of them spiritually from the evil that surrounded them.

The awesome act that followed Rahab's confession of faith was a mutual spiritual and physical rescue. In other words, as long as they remained faithful, Rahab and the spies became God's agents to rescue each other. It began when Rahab called on the spies for a favor.

> Now therefore, I pray you, swear unto me by the Lord, since I have shewed you kindness, that ye will also shew kindness unto my father's house, and give me a true token: And that ye will save alive my father, and my mother, and my brethren, and my sisters, and all that they have, and deliver our lives from death (Josh 2:12–13).

Rahab asked them to pledge ("give me a true token") to rescue her family from the utter destruction that she expected when the Israelites attacked. Rahab asked for a favor from the spies that they could not grant, at least not in the way that she asked it.

Rahab was what the Israelites called a "stranger." Ever since the beginning of the exodus, "strangers" or what later became known as proselytes, were only conditionally accepted by the Israelites as believers.

> And when a stranger shall sojourn with thee, and will keep the passover to the Lord, let all his males be circumcised, and then let him come near and keep it; and he shall be as one that is born in the land: for no uncircumcised person shall eat thereof (Exod 12:48).

Gentile men who wished to convert to faith in God had to obey the commandments and laws of God, including circumcision. Gentile women faced no such constraint as circumcision, but certainly, they had to make their belief in God known and follow all commands and laws. Rahab had confessed her faith before witnesses, but her father and brothers, and any other males in her household, would not be eligible to be religious brethren until the next Passover. Further, her family was a family of Canaanites, who by the command of God were to be driven out of the land or destroyed. How were the spies to answer Rahab?

They too were in a dilemma: Either sin by swearing 'so help me God' to the rescue of this Canaanite family, or sin by failing to obey the command to "spy out the land, even Jericho." They insightfully resolved their dilemma by an oath that neither invoked God nor directly agreed to her demand: "And the men answered her, Our life for yours, if ye utter not this our business. And it shall be, when the Lord hath given us the land, that we will deal kindly and truly with thee" (Josh 2:14). Their reply was not an agreement but a counter-proposal.

In the negotiation, the spies had to maintain their own faithfulness. They made two promises to Rahab, both of which respected God's commands. First, they pledged their lives to protect her because she had protected them. They did not "swear by the Lord" because it would have been a pledge to violate a command to destroy the Canaanites in their land. They pledged their own lives, however, that they would protect her from harm. Second, they promised to deal honestly and "kindly" with her after the Israelites won the victory over Jericho. They did not mention her family. This counter-proposal fell short of what Rahab had asked for, but neither did its promises display any disobedience to God's commands. The spies remained faithful.

Rahab said nothing in response, but she trusted the spies to be faithful to their promises. She let the spies

> down by a cord through the window: for her house was upon the town wall, and she dwelt upon the wall. And she said unto them, Get you to the mountain, lest the pursuers meet you; and hide yourselves there three days, until the pursuers be returned: and afterward may ye go your way (Josh 2:15–16).

These commands were a sequenced set of instructions for their combined spiritual and physical rescue. She was the human instrument of God to rescue the spies from sin (i.e., the failure of their mission) as well as their lives from death through capture. The spiritual and physical rescues occurred at the same time, during the three days on the mountain.

If you look at the mountain today, you see how its elevation would have given the spies a view not only of the surrounding country but inside the city itself (see Figure 2). By following Rahab's instructions, the spies could both complete their mission and escape their pursuers. The spies received a double rescue typical of what we would expect from a rescue of the faithful from sin and death.

Figure 2. Entering Modern-Day Jericho from the South

When the spies reached the ground at the bottom of the rope, Rahab still had only the two promises from them that they had given to her earlier—to protect her during the battle, and after the battle, to deal with her kindly. They had agreed to rescue her, but what of her family? Based only on their faith that God would be merciful to her family, the spies gave Rahab detailed instructions so that they could be saved as well as she. Again, the commands were a sequenced set of instructions for a combined spiritual and physical rescue:

> Behold, when we come into the land, thou shalt bind this line of scarlet thread ["cord," NASB] in the window which thou didst let us down by: and thou shalt bring thy father, and thy mother, and thy brethren, and all thy father's household, home unto thee. And it shall be, that whosoever shall go out of the doors of thy house into the street, his blood shall be upon his head, and we will be guiltless: and whosoever shall be with thee in the house, his blood shall be on our head, if any hand be upon him. And if thou utter this our business, then we will be quit of thine oath which thou hast made us to swear (Josh 2:18–20).

This agreement was more comprehensive than the first, but by pledging their lives rather than making a vow to God, they remained obedient to God with respect to her family, whom God had not authorized them to rescue. Rahab made no vocal response to their first offer, which was for them to rescue her only, but she voiced agreement to this second offer. "And she said, According unto your words, so be it" (2:21). All Rahab had to do was to follow faithfully the commands for the rescue and believe in the spies' promises. In the end, her family did all the things that it was commanded to do.

We learn that the spies were also obedient to the commands that Rahab gave to them. "And they went, and came unto the mountain, and abode there three days, until the pursuers were returned: and the pursuers sought them throughout all the way, but found them not" (2:22). Three days gave the spies an opportunity to complete their mission. From the mountain, they could "view the land, even Jericho," which to this point, they had been unable to see. Their spiritual rescue (obeying the commands of their mission) was simultaneous with their physical rescue (staying in the mountain). After three days, they returned uneventfully to the Israelite camp.

The spies reported to Joshua that "Truly the Lord hath delivered into our hands all the land; for even all the inhabitants of the country do faint because of us" (2:24). They repeated to Joshua what Rahab had told them about the Canaanites (2:9). The spies' report was also similar to the report that Joshua and Caleb gave the Israelite people 38 years before. One wonders if Joshua recollected his earlier report and smiled: "their defense is departed from them, and the Lord is with us" (Num 14:9).

Joshua believed the spies, and the Israelites crossed the Jordan to begin to possess Canaan. Before they crossed over, Joshua had all of the male children circumcised who were born since the exodus began (Josh 5:7); and God "rolled away the reproach of Egypt from off you" (5:9). God freed them from the consequences of the unbelief of their parents, and Israel kept the Passover (5:10). As Joshua approached Jericho, he encountered the "captain of the host of the Lord" (5:14) as a sign from God that God would be with him in the following battle.

God gave Joshua instructions for the battle. The Israelite army was to circle Jericho for six days, preceded by priests sounding trumpets, who were to be followed by the ark of the covenant. On the seventh day, to sound the attack, the warriors were to shout, and "the wall of the city shall fall down flat, and the people shall ascend up every man straight before him" (Josh 6:5). Joshua followed the Lord's commands exactly as they were given, and just moments before the attack, he said,

> Shout; for the Lord hath given you the city. And the city shall be accursed, even it, and all that are therein, to the Lord: only Rahab the harlot shall live, she and all that are with her in the house, because she hid the messengers that we sent (6:16–17).

Joshua ordered Rahab and her family to be saved because she hid the spies, but God rescued her (and her family) from death in the collapse of the wall because she was faithful. Like the spies, she was rescued spiritually and physically at the same time because of her righteousness. Unlike the spies, her physical rescue was a miracle. She and her family both survived the collapse of the wall on which she lived.

In the account of Joshua, we learn about the faith of the Israelites that led to the destruction of Jericho. "So the people shouted when the priests blew with the trumpets: and it came to pass, when the people heard the sound of the trumpet, and the people shouted with a great shout, that the wall fell down flat" (6:20). God had commanded the destruction of the Canaanites (Deut 7:2), which is what Joshua did at Jericho:

> And they utterly destroyed all that was in the city, both man and woman, young and old, and ox, and sheep, and ass, with the edge of the sword. But Joshua had said unto the two men that had spied out the country, Go into the harlot's house, and bring out thence the woman, and all that she hath, as ye sware unto her (Josh 6:21–22).

Joshua sent the spies into the city to rescue her, their having earlier pledged their lives to protect her and her family.

> And the young men that were spies went in, and brought out Rahab, and her father, and her mother, and her brethren, and all that she had; and they brought out all her kindred, and left them without the camp of Israel (6:23).

The spies found her and her family exactly where they told them to be.

The Old Testament account tells us that Rahab and her family were physically rescued by Joshua and the spies. The New Testament adds that the reason that they were rescued was her faithfulness: "By faith the walls of Jericho fell down, after they were compassed about seven days. By faith the harlot Rahab perished not with them that believed not, when she had received the spies with peace" (Heb 11:30–31). The same faithfulness of the Israelites that led to the miraculous fall of the walls of Jericho led to the miraculous preservation of Rahab and her family. Neither she nor her family died with the unbelievers.

Rahab and her family were left outside the Israelite camp. Why? Being left outside the camp was the equivalent of being declared unclean. It was a place where people were sent for purification. What Rahab had done for God, the spies, and the other Israelites made her fully acceptable to God, but her father and her brothers had not been circumcised; therefore, they could not be accepted in the camp by the Israelites. Because the Israelites had just celebrated Passover, Rahab and her family probably resided outside the camp for a year, and the males in the family were circumcised immediately before the next Passover as they too became proselytes.

The book of Joshua leaves Rahab dwelling among the Israelites because of her good work of hiding the spies: "And Joshua saved Rahab the harlot alive, and her father's household, and all that she had; and she dwelleth in Israel even unto this day; because she hid the messengers, which Joshua sent to spy out Jericho" (Josh 6:25). Ending at the time that Joshua wrote, Rahab's story was incomplete. She was accepted by the Israelites as a proselyte, but her acceptance was based on what she had done rather than who she had become. Despite her sinful past as a Canaanite, a prostitute, the keeper of a brothel and a deceiver, she had become a model of faith. John MacArthur has written that "the disturbing fact about what she once *was* simply magnifies the glory of divine grace, which is what made her the extraordinary woman that she *became*."[1]

God would have the last word in her story. In the New Testament genealogy of Joseph, the husband of Mary and father of Jesus, there is a reference to a woman named "Rachab" (Matt 1:5; "Rehab" NASB). She is one of only five women listed in the ancestry of Jesus Christ. Matthew's mention of Rahab as an ancestor of Christ honors her, as do the references to her faithfulness by the writer of the book of Hebrews and by James, the brother of Jesus, but there is more.

When Rahab became an obedient believer, she gave up her earlier lifestyle. The genealogy of Christ tells us that she married Salmon, who was the son of Naasson (Matt 1:4). Naasson was Aaron's brother-in-law and the leader of the tribe of Judah at the time of the exodus (Exod 6:23; Num 7:11–12). Both at the time of the exodus and at the time of the attack on Jericho, Judah was the largest of the twelve tribes of Israel. Naasson died in the desert along with his generation. His son, Salmon, was between 20 and 40 years old when the Israelites attacked Jericho. Some people speculate that Salmon was one of the two spies whom Rahab saved and who pledged their lives for hers. Salmon fits the role of someone who could have been selected as a spy—a young, probably unmarried man who was known for his faithfulness to God—but we cannot determine from the Bible whether or not he was one of the two who spied out the land.

Today, Christians do not send out spies, but they do send out teachers in obedience to the Great Commission: "Go ye therefore, and teach all nations, baptizing them in the name of the Father, and of the Son, and of the Holy Ghost: Teaching them to observe all things whatsoever I have commanded you" (Matt 28:19–20). Missionaries are sent in obedience to the commands to "go" and "teach" often in places where non-belief, straying belief and even unbelief are common. Sometimes they are surrounded by unbelievers and are in danger. They may even be accused of spying.

What should the faithful do if danger approaches, and they are helpless to extract themselves from the situation or even to contact support? One thing faithful Christians can always do is pray for a spiritual rescue. Jesus ended the Lord's prayer, "And lead us not into temptation, but deliver us from evil: For thine is the kingdom, and the power, and the glory, for ever. Amen" (Matt 6:13). What is a prayer to God to "deliver us from evil" but a prayer by the faithful for a spiritual rescue from surrounding sin? The Israelite spies received such a rescue from God through Rahab, and Rahab received such a rescue from God through the spies. The wisdom of Albert Barnes, cited in Chapter 2, is worth repeating:

He can send an angel to take his tempted people by the hand; he can interpose and destroy the power of the tempter; he can raise up earthly friends; he can deliver his people completely and forever from temptation, by their removal to heaven.[2]

God can use any means to rescue the faithful from sin and death. The task of the faithful is to remain faithful during the rescue by following the commands for the rescue, as did both Rahab and the spies. A quick review of cases suggests that detailed obedience to rescue commands leads to a successful rescue (as in the case of Job), whereas even partial disobedience to the rescue commands results in a failed rescue (as in the case of Lot).

What Christians can learn from Rahab is just as important as what they can learn from the spies. Through his marriage to Rahab, Salmon brought Rahab into the center of the largest and most praiseworthy family of Israel (Gen 49:8). Rahab was no longer "the harlot." She became the mother of Boaz (Matt 1:5), who was kind, honest and faithful, which were characteristics that seem to reflect the traits of both Salmon and Rahab. Using the spies as well as His own miraculous powers, God rescued Rahab from a sinful past to occupy a position of honor within the tribe of Judah and within the ancestry of Jesus.

The story of Rahab reveals the power of a spiritual rescue to transform a life. After her belief and obedience, God rescued her from a sinful life; then as a faithful woman, He rescued her from a sinful city and the collapse of her house. She carried out all that she had (Josh 6:23), but more important than anything else was her new faith, and God set her on a path to prominence and prosperity. Would her transformation have occurred had she not first found herself in a desperate situation? We cannot say, but often desperate situations are necessary before people are willing to let go of their sinful lifestyle, believe in God and obey Him. "With God," said Jesus, "all things are possible" (Matt 19:26). With God, there is always hope of salvation.

STUDY QUESTIONS

1. Many people feel left out by society. They are on the margins, much like Rahab while she lived in Jericho. When is life "on the margins" an advantage?
2. Making an oath is so common in the story of Rahab that it must have special meaning. Why are promises so important in this story?
3. Almost every day, we are challenged to be kind and to tell the truth at the same time. Give a recent example when you were challenged to do both (to be kind and to tell the truth). Did you succeed? If not, what could you have done differently?
4. Conversion to Christianity involves hearing the word of

God, believing it, repenting of sin, confessing Jesus as the Son of God, being baptized for forgiveness of sins, and living a faithful life. Outline a similar process in the conversion of Rahab to Judaism.

5. God has the power to transform us in ways that we cannot transform ourselves. His transformation of "Rahab the harlot" into a model of faithfulness is one example. Can you think of a similar example of transformation in the New Testament?

9

RESCUE FROM MULTIPLE SINS

David

And it came to pass in an eveningtide, that David arose from off his bed, and walked upon the roof of the king's house: and from the roof he saw a woman washing herself; and the woman was very beautiful to look upon. And David sent and inquired after the woman. And one said, Is not this Bathsheba, the daughter of Eliam, the wife of Uriah the Hittite? (2 Sam 11:2–3)

God had commanded: "Thou shalt not covet thy neighbour's house, thou shalt not covet thy neighbour's wife, nor his manservant, nor his maidservant, nor his ox, nor his ass, nor any thing that is thy neighbour's" (Exod 20:17). What led David to break this commandment and covet Bathsheba, his neighbor's wife? What made a rescue from sin necessary for the chief judge of Israel after he was reminded whose she was?

THE CAUSE OF DAVID'S SIN

Part of the answer is at the beginning of the story.

And it came to pass, after the year was expired, at the time when kings go forth to battle, that David sent Joab, and his servants with him, and all Israel; and they destroyed the children of Ammon, and besieged Rabbah. But David tarried still at Jerusalem (2 Sam 11:1).

David was king of Israel. In the spring, David sent his chief military commander, Joab, with the Israelite army to attack the Ammonites and lay siege to Rabbah, their principal city (where Amman, Jordan is today), but David was not where he should have been. He should have been with Joab and the army.

What was David doing in Jerusalem? "And it came to pass in an eveningtide, that David arose from off his bed, and walked upon the roof of the king's house." (11:2). David had spent the afternoon in his bed and went for a walk on the roof of the palace. He was not ill. He was not doing anything purposeful that evening. David was idle, both physically and mentally.

Idleness is not the same as rest. Idleness is a form of relaxation in which people give themselves over to their natural tendencies. Have you ever heard the saying, 'idle hands are the devil's workshop?' It sounds biblical, but it is not. Nevertheless, this popular proverb expresses a truth. When people allow themselves to be idle, both physically and mentally, they drop their guard against all their natural tendencies, including temptations. They do not intend to sin, but they become vulnerable to whatever temptation comes to mind as a fantasy or is in front of them. "Every man is tempted, when he is drawn away of his own lust, and enticed. Then when lust hath conceived, it bringeth forth sin: and sin, when it is finished, bringeth forth death" (James 1:14–15). In David's case, he saw a beautiful woman, bathing in the twilight. Rather than turn away, he watched her, and he lusted after her.

When David heard that she belonged to Uriah, he had already sinned. Satan's trap had sprung, and David was caught. When David coveted what he saw, he broke the commandment, "thou shalt not covet thy neighbour's wife." Had he stopped there, his sin would have been serious enough, but he broke two more commandments. "David sent messengers, and took her; and she came in unto him, and he lay with her; for she was purified from her uncleanness: and she returned unto her house (2 Sam 11:4). During that day, wives were considered the property of their husbands. By taking Bathsheba from Uriah's house, David broke the command "Thou shalt not steal" (Exod 20:15). The theft of Bathsheba from Uriah was possible because Uriah was with the Israelite army at Rabbah. Further, when David lay with her, he broke a third commandment: "Thou shalt not commit adultery" (Exod 20:14).

The matter went from bad to worse. Within a few weeks, Bathsheba discovered that she was with child and informed David, leading him to attempt to conceal the source of the pregnancy. He plotted to deceive Uriah into believing that the child was his own. He called Uriah home from the siege, pretended to seek news of its progress and dismissed Uriah home to rest, hoping that Uriah would lay with Bathsheba. Inadvertently, Uriah spoiled David's plot when he refused to enter his house, and instead, he slept with the king's servants at the door of the palace. When asked by David why he would not go home, Uriah replied,

> The ark, and Israel, and Judah, abide in tents; and my lord Joab, and the servants of my lord, are encamped in the open fields; shall I then go into mine house, to eat and to drink, and to lie with my wife? as thou livest, and as thy soul liveth, I will not do this thing (2 Sam 11:11).

Uriah promised that he would not lie with his wife while his brothers in arms were in the field. He had a compassion for his fellow soldiers in the field that David did not have or else David would have been there with them.

David's only concern at this point was to cover up his sins against Uriah. In desperation, David sent Uriah back to the army with a letter to Joab that read, "Set ye Uriah in the forefront of the hottest battle, and retire ye from him, that he may be smitten, and die" (11:15). Joab did as the king commanded. David had broken a fourth commandment: "Thou shalt not kill" (Exod 20:13). Uriah was dead, and after Bathsheba mourned, David married her. In the matter of Uriah the Hittite, David had broken four out of six commandments that God had made for the good of humanity in dealings with itself. The cause? A lack of compassion that led him to be absent from the army and idle in Jerusalem. All of his sins broke the great commandment, "Love thy neighbour as thyself" (Lev. 19:18). Uriah was his next-door neighbor.

THE STORY OF TWO RESCUES

There were two rescues of David, one within the other. The story with the larger scope is the spiritual rescue of David from a lack of compassion for his neighbor Uriah, which caused all of his other sins. Had David followed the commandment "thou shalt love thy neighbor as thyself," he never would have sinned against Uriah. He would have had compassion on him, and he would have left Bathsheba alone. As correction, David had to learn through suffering to be compassionate when the circumstances allowed for it, even with his enemies. The story of spiritual rescue from a lack of compassion for his neighbor is largely told through 2 Samuel, Chapters 11 through 13.

The other story of rescue has a narrower scope: Rescue from the sentence of death. This story is largely told through a series of four penitential psalms (6, 38, 51 and 32). This series noted by Franz Delitzsch traced David's progression from unbelief to obedient belief, with corresponding reflections on his health.[1] If David wrote these psalms, and if they were about his punishment for willful sin, they could only have been about the incidents that led up to and followed the murder of Uriah, "Because David did that which was right in the eyes of the Lord, and turned not aside from any thing that he commanded him all the days of his life, save only in the matter of Uriah the Hittite" (1 Kgs 15:5). As chief judge of Israel, David knew that he deserved to die for committing adultery with Bathsheba and for planning the murder of Uriah. We can infer that God condemned him to death because David felt himself dying from his sin. With a dying body and a troubled mind, David humbled himself and prayed to God for salvation. God would release David from death, but not before David demonstrated his love for Him and repentance.

Despite their location in different parts of the Bible, the stories of the two rescues are closely related. The first two psalms (6 and 38) concern events *before* David confessed his sin in 2 Samuel 12:13. Psalm 51 concerns David's confession and repentance, and Psalm 32, the forgiveness of God for his sin. The close relationship between the two stories does not prevent us from analyzing them as rescues from sin and death, but it does require us to pay close attention to the details of each and how they relate to each other to develop a better understanding of what happened.

A DYING BODY AND A TROUBLED MIND

After David murdered Uriah, his health declined enough so that he was concerned about his impending death. He needed a physical rescue. David interpreted the worsening condition of his body as a reflection of the state of his soul. He feared that he was dying, and that the cause was God's anger directed against him.

> O Lord, rebuke me not in thine anger, neither chasten me in thy hot displeasure. Have mercy upon me, O Lord; for I am weak: O Lord, heal me; for my bones are vexed. My soul is also sore vexed: but thou, O Lord, how long? (Psalm 6:1–3)

David prayed to God to end His anger and begin to heal him, both physically and spiritually. "Return, O Lord, deliver my soul: oh save me for thy mercies' sake. For in death there is no remembrance of thee: in the grave who shall give thee thanks?" (vv. 4–5). David had confidence that God had heard his weeping and his prayer for mercy and health. "The Lord hath heard my supplication; the Lord will receive my prayer" (v. 9). His first prayer ended with a plea for relief from his enemies: "Let all mine enemies be ashamed and sore vexed" (v. 10). He was confident that God heard his prayer, and he waited for an answer.

David had not dealt with his sin through prayer, even though he interpreted God's anger as the source of his physical deterioration. He had only asked for a rescue from his physical, spiritual, and social ills. He had not dealt with the cause of God's anger towards him. For a person who was righteous, his prayer for a rescue from ill health and his enemies would have been totally appropriate, but David was not righteous. He was deeply in sin, which apparently was the cause of God's anger and punishment.

God did not answer his prayer. We know from Psalm 38 that his physical, spiritual, and social conditions did not improve because he began his prayer to God with almost the same words as Psalm 6: "O Lord, rebuke me not in thy wrath: neither chasten me in thy hot displeasure" (Psalm 38:1). God's anger could only be due to David's sins in the matter of Uriah. No other incident in David's life displeased God.

As David became aware of the cause of God's anger, he returned to prayer for help with his sin, acknowledging that his illness was God's punishment. "For thine arrows stick fast in me, and thy hand presseth me sore" (v. 2). God would not punish the righteous so. His physical, spiritual and social conditions worsened to the point that he could neither gain strength nor sleep because of constant restlessness: "There is no soundness in my flesh because of thine anger; neither is there any rest in my bones *because of my sin*" (v. 3, emphasis added). For the first time, David addressed his unforgiven sin as the cause of his suffering. He did not describe the sin. It could have been his adultery with Bathsheba, his murder of Uriah, or either of the other sins associated with these two, both of which were worthy of death. His sin could also have been the intentionality or willfulness involved in murder, which was also worthy of death. If anything, David had become more bowed down with the weight of his multiple sins. "As an heavy burden they are too heavy for me. My wounds stink and are corrupt because of my foolishness" (vv. 4–5). In each verse, he blamed his illness on his "foolishness" or manifold sins.

Even as David weakened, his friends avoided him and his enemies increased in strength.

> My lovers and my friends stand aloof from my sore; and my kinsmen stand afar off. They also that seek after my life lay snares for me: and they that seek my hurt speak mischievous things, and imagine deceits all the day long (vv. 11–12).

Likely sources of his worsening social conditions were both his disease, which not even his friends wanted to see, and his sins, which may have been known by his enemies as well as his friends. His sins "hast given great occasion to the enemies of the Lord to blaspheme" (2 Sam 12:14). David now knew that something about him would have to change to avoid death either from disease or from his enemies. From all appearances, God would not save him in his unrighteous state.

At the center of this Psalm 38, David admitted to his helplessness to respond to the criticism from his friends and his enemies alike. "But I, as a deaf man, heard not; and I was as a dumb man that openeth not his mouth. Thus I was as a man that heareth not, and in whose mouth are no reproofs" (Psalm 38:13–14). He knew that he was guilty of intentional sin, and as Bathsheba's pregnancy progressed, he would soon be unable to deny it. Everyone had witnessed Uriah's refusal to sleep with Bathsheba while on leave from the army at the siege at Rabbah. Delitzsch commented about David that "In the consciousness of his sin he is obliged to be silent and, renouncing all self-help, to abandon his cause to God."[2] David humbled himself and admitted that he was helpless to save himself from death and the triumph of his enemies.

The last few verses of Psalm 38 contain an extraordinary spiritual insight. David discovered a spiritual path from unbelief to straying belief, which was a path no one whom we have studied had found before. All who had willfully sinned had died. The unbelieving inhabitants of the ancient world were drowned in the flood; the wicked inhabitants of Sodom and her four sister cities were destroyed in a hail of fire and brimstone; the rebellious generation of Israelites died in the desert; and the Canaanites of Jericho were all killed by Joshua and his army. Survivors were either righteous or (in the case of Lot) a straying believer, but never had an unbeliever been rescued from death for his or her intentional sin. All had been warned, but none had found the way to repentance from their spiritual condition of unbelief.

At the end of Psalm 38, David admitted to God that he had sinned intentionally, and he put himself at God's mercy. "For I am ready to halt, and my sorrow is continually before me. For I will declare mine iniquity; I will be sorry for my sin" (v. 17–18). Apparently, David did not know whether or not the Lord would abandon him for committing so many sins so deliberately. "Forsake me not, O Lord: O my God, be not far from me. Make haste to help me, O Lord my salvation" (vv. 21–22). We can hear David's utter dependance on God's mercy to help him in what must have been a terrifying spiritual situation. As Delitzsch pointed out, David had abandoned all thought of helping himself in Psalm 38. Through humility, prayer to God, and seeking a personal relationship with Him, David had found *the* path from unbelief to straying belief.

David still needed to repent, but Psalm 38 represents a turn towards God by an unbeliever *before* he turned away from sin. He put himself totally at God's mercy. This readiness to repent was his spiritual condition when the prophet Nathan showed up (in 2 Sam 12:1) with a case for David to hear in his court. Table 3 represents the process of turning to God that David had discovered out of the depths of his helplessness, his desire for salvation from intentional sin and his love for God

TABLE 3
THE PROCESS OF TURNING TO GOD

Process	Interpretation
Humble self	Recognize personal helplessness apart from God
Pray	Ask God to hear/answer prayers
Seek God	Develop personal relationship
Repent	See Table 2

The process of turning to God is a description of how someone returned to God after rejecting Him and His word. The process is not a prescription nor a checklist. Turning to God required David first to humble himself in response to punishment. As we have seen in other chapters of this book, many unbelievers would rather die before they humbled themselves, which is why David's achievement in Psalm 38 was so great. The king humbled himself in response to his pain. The process also required David to reach out in prayer to God, a demonstration of his desire to communicate with God. David reached out with promises of confession ("I will declare mine iniquity; I will be sorry for my sin"). Finally, the unbeliever must want a closer relationship to God. David pleaded for God to be close ("Forsake me not, O Lord: O my God, be not far from me"). All three of these acts were the initiative of David.

How do we know that God answered David's prayer in Psalm 38? God sent the prophet Nathan to bring about David's confession and to pronounce the judgments of God for what David had done. God responded to David's plea to his rescuer ("O Lord my salvation") with a rescue from sin and death.

DAVID'S CONFESSION

David had promised God that he would confess his sin, which would begin the process of repentance, but for one reason or another, David had not yet confessed when Nathan appeared in his court. Nathan brought a court case to David that would lead him to confess as part of his spiritual rescue:

> There were two men in one city; the one rich, and the other poor. The rich man had exceeding many flocks and herds: But the poor man had nothing, save one little ewe lamb, which he had bought and nourished up: and it grew up together with him, and with his children; it did eat of his own meat, and drank of his own cup, and lay in his bosom, and was unto him as a daughter. And there came a traveller unto the rich man, and he spared to take of his own flock and of his own herd, to dress for the wayfaring man that was come unto him; but took the poor man's lamb, and dressed it for the man that was come to him. (2 Sam 12:1–4).

Nathan mentioned no names, just a rich man (who represented David) with many "flocks and herds" (which represented his wives and concubines) and a poor man (who represented Uriah) with one ewe lamb (which represented Bathsheba). David reacted emotionally to hearing the case: "And David's anger was greatly kindled against the man; and he said to Nathan, As the Lord liveth, the man that hath done this thing shall surely die" (12:5). Death was a punishment more harsh than the sentence prescribed for theft: "If a man shall steal an ox, or a sheep, and kill it, or sell it; he shall restore five oxen for an ox, and four sheep for a sheep" (Exod 22:1). In his anger, David added the penalty of death to the appropriate restitution (four sheep) because the rich man "had no pity" or compassion for the poor man (2 Sam 12:6).

David was the rich man who had acted with no compassion for his neighbor Uriah. "And Nathan said to David, Thou art the man"

(12:7). Without waiting for a confession from David, Nathan pronounced God's judgments. Through Nathan, God asked David a rhetorical question, "Wherefore hast thou despised the commandment of the Lord, to do evil in his sight?" (2 Sam 12:9). The Hebrew word for "despised" (*bazah*) was the same word used by Moses to describe the attitude of willful or deliberate sinners, as opposed to sinners who broke commands out of ignorance (Num 15:22–29). God implied that that David had deliberately rejected God's commandments, or was someone we might call an unbeliever. "Because he hath despised [*bazah*] the word of the Lord, and hath broken his commandment, that soul shall utterly be cut off; his iniquity shall be upon him" (15:31). The judgment for despising God's commandments was clearly death, but God just as clearly refrained from imposing the death sentence on David for his willful sin. Instead, He judged David as a straying sinner.

Nathan continued to speak for God:

> Thou hast killed Uriah the Hittite with the sword, and hast taken his wife to be thy wife, and hast slain him with the sword of the children of Ammon. Now therefore the sword shall never depart from thine house; because thou hast despised [*bazah*] me, and hast taken the wife of Uriah the Hittite to be thy wife (2 Sam 12:9–10).

The sentence for murdering and stealing was a promise to trouble David's house by "the sword." Members of his family would die by being slashed or stabbed. David would suffer their loss in a way that reflected how Uriah had died in battle.

As for coveting Bathsheba and committing adultery, these sins were punished by a second part of God's sentence, which built upon the first:

> Thus saith the Lord, Behold, I will raise up evil against thee out of thine own house, and I will take thy wives before thine eyes, and give them unto thy neighbour, and he shall lie with thy wives in

the sight of this sun. For thou didst it secretly: but I will do this thing before all Israel, and before the sun (12:11–12)

or in broad daylight. Through these promises, God would allow the covetousness and adulterous lust of one of David's neighbors to victimize David as David had victimized his neighbor Uriah.

At this point, David confessed his sin.

And David said unto Nathan, I have sinned against the Lord. And Nathan said unto David, The Lord also hath put away thy sin; thou shalt not die. Howbeit, because by this deed thou hast given great occasion to the enemies of the Lord to blaspheme, the child also that is born unto thee shall surely die (2 Sam 12:13–14).

These words reflect less God's forgiveness than His mercy in commuting David's sentence from death to suffering appropriate consequences in life for his sins. These consequences began with the death of the baby conceived out of wedlock, born from adulterous parents, and the cause of blasphemy (speaking disrespectfully about God), a form of unbelief.

Why did God commute David's sentence? Why did he rescue him from death? We may never know, but some of his extraordinary circumstances may have made his sin forgivable. The first was his readiness to confess. In Psalm 38 he all but confessed of his willful sin. He had turned to God for both a spiritual and a physical rescue. He knew that he was guilty of a terrible sin—most recently described as "despising" the commandments of God—which led to other sins that in themselves were worthy of death. But with awareness of his intentional sin, he had worked out his own salvation "with fear and trembling" (Phil 2:12) by voluntarily returning to God, as we saw in Psalm 38. This spiritual development occurred before Nathan stepped foot in David's court and announced God's judgments.

A second reason why God was more likely to commute David's

sentence from death to suffering in life was David's position as king. God had elevated him to be king from being a common man with a heart for God. "The Lord seeth not as man seeth; for man looketh on the outward appearance, but the Lord looketh on the heart" (1 Sam 16:7). In other words, God chose David as "a man after mine own heart" (Acts 13:22). God chose someone who could be humble and learn to be a good king for His people, which appears to be what God decided to teach him through corrective punishments for his sins.

A third reason why God might have commuted his death sentence was His use for David, not just as a king, but as the ancestor of Jesus, who descended from Solomon.

> And there shall come forth a rod out of the stem of Jesse, and a Branch shall grow out of his roots: And the spirit of the Lord shall rest upon him, the spirit of wisdom and understanding, the spirit of counsel and might, the spirit of knowledge and of the fear of the Lord (Isa 11:1–2).

Jesse was the father of David. The Messiah would come through the lineage of David and even be called "the son of David" (Matt 1:1; Mark 10:47) David's son Solomon was the ancestor of Joseph, the earthly father of Jesus. Solomon would have never been born had David died for his sins shortly after he had confessed them.

For one reason or another, David was spared the death penalty. David had confessed, and he had heard the sentences against him, including the death of his first son by Bathsheba, but he had still not fully repented of his sins. He had not completed what he knew he had to do in order to be forgiven, if forgiveness was possible

DAVID'S REPENTANCE

Table 2 in Chapter 3 of this book presented a description of repentance developed from what Elihu taught Job. The elements of repentance included an admission of guilt (e.g., "I have sinned"), a description of the sin (e.g., "I have perverted that which was right") and penitence (e.g., "it profited me not"). We are familiar with these terms with perhaps the exception of *penitence,* which is "the action of feeling or showing sorrow and regret for having done wrong" (*Oxford English Dictionary*). Although David confessed his sin in front of Nathan (and probably in front of his court), he had not described his sin. Nor had he demonstrated his regret for having sinned, which in Mosaic law, was accomplished through vows (e.g., to repay what was stolen) and sacrifices.

David must have written Psalm 51 shortly after he confessed his sin. The psalm was inscribed, "of David, when Nathan the prophet came unto him, after he had gone in to Bath-sheba." It began with a prayer for the forgiveness of his sin, and it ended with vows to please God. He began by confessing his sin and describing it in various ways:

> Have mercy upon me, O God, according to thy lovingkindness: according unto the multitude of thy tender mercies blot out my transgressions. Wash me thoroughly from mine iniquity, and cleanse me from my sin. For I acknowledge my transgressions: my sin is ever before me (Psalm 51:1–3).

In the first three verses, David not only repeatedly owned "my transgressions," "mine iniquity," and "my sin," but he used three different words to describe it, each with its own meaning. A "transgression" (*pesha*) is a "revolt" or rebellion, willful infringement or trespass. A transgression involves a breaking of trust and a departure from God. "Iniquity" (*avon* or *avown*) is from "perversity," or a moral uncleanness. Iniquity involves crookedness in the character of a person. A "sin" (*chattath*) is a a common failure (as in "missing the mark"). The most common spiritual failures are failures to love God and others. Using the words "transgressions," "iniquity," and "sin," David described the different types of sin in which he had been engaged in the matter of Uriah. They included his departures from God (transgressions), which were intentional; sins of moral character (iniquity), such as adultery and murder; and failure to love his neighbor (sin), that is, his failure to have compassion for Uriah. David described his sin in all its complexity, if not in all its details.

What remained of his repentance was feeling and showing regret for what he had done. We can hear the echoes of his transgressions, his iniquity, and his sin in his plea: "Create in me a clean heart, O God; and renew a right spirit within me. Cast me not away from thy presence; and take not thy holy spirit from me. Restore unto me the joy of thy salvation; and uphold me with thy free spirit" (vv 10–12). In these verses, David no longer described his sin. Rather, he pleaded for a rescue from his sin ("the joy of thy salvation"), implying his regret for what he had done. Without the hope of a rescue, he would have been left in the condition from which he prayed to God he could escape.

David had a spiritual insight at this point in his repentance. He spiritualized his sacrifice to atone for trespasses for which, ironically, there was no atonement. "For thou desirest not sacrifice; else would I give it: thou delightest not in burnt offering. The sacrifices of God are a broken spirit: a broken and a contrite heart, O God, thou wilt not despise [*bazah*]" (vv. 16–17). David's repentance matched his trespasses, which, because of their intentionality, had "despised" God. From his love of God, he believed that God would not despise the offer of his inner state of sorrow (a broken heart) and regret (a contrite heart). Out of such a heart, had his sins been unintentional, burnt offerings might be appropriate. Unlike burnt offerings, however, spiritual offerings endure. David's offering was neither incomplete nor temporary. He would approach many events later in life with a "broken and contrite" heart.

David included in Psalm 51 a vow to "teach transgressors thy ways; and sinners shall be converted unto thee" (v. 13). These promises were fulfilled in Psalm 32, in which David celebrated God's rescue from sin and physical affliction: "I acknowledged my sin unto thee, and mine iniquity have I not hid. I said, I will confess my transgressions unto the Lord; and thou forgavest the iniquity of my sin" (v. 5). David told sinners and obedient believers alike that a rescue exists for the faithful from sin and death:

> For this [spiritual and physical rescue] shall every one that is godly pray unto thee in a time when thou mayest be found [of spiritual danger and helplessness]: surely in the floods of great waters [as in Noah's day] they shall not come nigh unto him. Thou art my hiding place; thou shalt preserve me from trouble; thou shalt compass me about with songs of deliverance [or rescue] (vv. 6–7).

If the godly pray for a rescue when they need one, God will provide one. Here is the second place in the Old Testament that we have found a description of God's offer to the faithful of a rescue from sin and death.[3]

God spared David from death because he had found his way back from unbelief to obedient belief, but the commutation of the death sentence also allowed David time to become a better king. Adopting the persona of God in Psalm 32, David wrote,

> I will instruct thee and teach thee in *the* way which thou shalt go: I will guide thee with mine eye. Be ye not as the horse, or as the mule, which have no understanding: whose mouth must be held in with bit and bridle, lest they come near unto thee (32:8–9, emphasis added).

Reconciled with God, David would not escape His sentences for sins, but at the same time God promised to continue to teach David "the way" of salvation. The God who had punished him would now instruct him, through suffering, to become compassionate. David would later say, "The Lord hath chastened me sore: but he hath not given me over unto death" (Psalm 118:18).

Through his own rescue from sin and death, David discovered

that an offer of rescue by God extends to the unbeliever, as astonishing as that discovery at first may seem. The unbeliever has to do his or her part in the rescue, but the offer is not limited to the godly. Unlike the godly, the unbeliever must first turn to God before being rescued from sin (Psalm 32). Even then, the formerly unbelieving person has not become godly. He or she must repent of sin to be rescued from sin (Psalm 51). The extra step is necessary because an unbeliever is, in a figurative sense, twice lost. Once they seek and find God, then they must repent of their sins before they can be faithful or godly.

Unbelievers are like people completely lost in the woods. Normally, people lost in the woods can find their way out by retracing their steps, but what if they become so disoriented that they cannot retrace their steps? What do they do then? Because of their unbelief, they cannot simply repent (turn around and retrace their steps). The choices around them for which direction to take are infinite. They must first orient themselves to *something,* whether it is a landmark, the direction of the sun, or the side of trees on which moss grows. To escape intentional sin, the unbeliever needs to orient to God. Literally, that is what "orient" means, to face east. Once the unbeliever has oriented to God, he or she becomes a straying believer, someone who is still lost, but who can find their way out of sin through repentance because of their belief in God. Frequently, they follow His commands, but David's personal discovery of the path back to obedient belief and to life was an extraordinary spiritual achievement because he did not have to follow commands. He followed the love of God in his heart.

IMPLICATION FOR CHRISTIANS

The process of turning to God involved humbling oneself, praying to God, and seeking a closer relationship with God *before* repenting of sin. In short, it involved total dependance on God's mercy for a spiritual rescue. This process would later be described by God to

Solomon at the dedication of the Temple: "If my people, which are called by my name, shall humble themselves, and pray, and seek my face, and turn from their wicked ways; then I will hear from heaven, and will forgive their sin, and will heal their land" (2 Chron 7:14). God promised to forgive their deliberate sin, if in humility, they sought a closer relationship with Him *before* they repented of their sins ("wicked ways"). Jonah would follow a similar process to escape from death itself, and the Ninevites would rely on it to avoid total destruction (see Chapter 11). As mentioned earlier, the Hebrew writer warned Hebrew Christians, "Take heed, brethren, lest there be in any of you an evil heart of unbelief, in departing from the living God" (Heb 3:12), but with David, we also see that "with God all things are possible" (Matt 19:26). Even unbelievers who want to repent of sin can repent if they put themselves at the mercy of God in the form of Jesus Christ, who has come to rescue everyone from sin, not just the godly, the non-believer, or the straying believer. He came to rescue unbelievers as well.

Paul is perhaps our best example. He told Timothy, "This is a faithful saying, and worthy of all acceptation, that Christ Jesus came into the world to save sinners; of whom I am chief" (1 Tim 1:15). As "chiefest of sinners," Paul (or Saul, as he was then known) was an unbeliever in Jesus Christ as the Son of God. "As for Saul, he made havock of the church, entering into every house, and haling men and women committed them to prison. Therefore they that were scattered abroad went every where preaching the word" (Acts 8:3–4). Saul as an unbeliever persecuted and punished obedient believers, but God used him as a tool to seed "the word" in places distant from Jerusalem.

Saul was still "breathing out threatenings and slaughter against the disciples of the Lord" (Acts 9:1) when he left Jerusalem to persecute obedient Christians in Damascus. Jesus, who had already ascended to heaven, called out to him on the road. Saul had a blinding vision "And he trembling and astonished said, Lord, what wilt thou have me to do? And the Lord said unto him, Arise, and go into the city, and it shall be told thee what thou must do" (9:6). Paul humbled himself and put himself completely at the mercy of Jesus. He did out of faith in Jesus Christ what he was commanded to do ("Arise" and "go into the city"). Even unbelievers have been rescued from their unbelief, if they turned to Jesus.

STUDY QUESTIONS

1. When kings go to war, David was in Jerusalem and his army was camped 45 miles away. How did Uriah show greater compassion for the suffering of his brothers in arms than did David?
2. In 2 Samuel 12:13, David confesses "I have sinned against the Lord" *before* Nathan tells him that "The Lord hath also put away thy sin" (v. 13). Do you think that the sequence of these two events is significant? What could it signify?
3. God would later give to Solomon, the son of David, a key to unlock the door firmly shut between God and a willful sinner. Read 2 Chronicles 7:14 and cite verses from Psalm 38 to show that David found the "key" that opened the door of repentance to unbelievers.
4. How can a "broken and contrite heart" grow compassion (literally, the ability to "suffer with" someone)? Develop a realistic example.
5. Have you ever met someone who believed that they could not be rescued from their sins? How did you respond? Where would you go in the Bible to begin a study?

10

RESCUE FROM FEAR

Elijah

And he was afraid and got up and ran for his life and came to Beersheba, which belongs to Judah; and left his servant there. But he himself went a day's journey into the wilderness, and came and sat down under a broom tree; and he asked for himself to die (1 Kgs 19:3–4 NASB).

Elijah was a prophet of Israel who lived during the reign of Ahab, the seventh king of Israel (or the Northern Kingdom).[1] Ahab married Jezebel, the daughter of the king of Sidon (or Zidon), a city on the coast of the Mediterranean Sea, north of Israel. Ahab began to worship Jezebel's god, Baal. Ahab "did more to provoke the Lord God of Israel to anger than all the kings of Israel that were before him" (1 Kgs 16:33). Elijah stepped into the picture to confront Ahab with a prophecy of punishment for Israel, but after Ahab and Israel repented, we find Elijah frightened and alone in the desert, wishing to die. What frightened him so, and how did God rescue him from his fear?

To understand why Elijah was so frightened, we need to go back to the beginning of his story. Elijah appeared in Ahab and Jezebel's court in the city of Samaria one day to make an important prophecy. "And Elijah the Tishbite, who was of the inhabitants of Gilead, said unto Ahab, As the Lord God of Israel liveth, before whom I stand, there shall not be dew nor rain these years, but according to my word" (1 Kgs 17:1). Elijah was from Gilead, an area on the East Bank of the Jordan River. The East Bank was then under the control of the Israelites. Promising his king that it would not rain 'until I say otherwise' was a dangerous message to bring to court, but Ahab initially seems to have dismissed it, as well as Elijah. As Jesus would later remark about Elijah (and Himself), "Verily I say unto you, No prophet is accepted in his own country" (Luke 4:24). Ahab had already shown that he did not believe in God, so why should he believe this prophet from nowhere? Ahab's initial unbelief afforded Elijah an opportunity to hide so that he could not be found when Ahab decided to look for him (1 Kgs 18:10).

God commanded Elijah where to go to hide. "Get thee hence, and turn thee eastward, and hide thyself by the brook Cherith, that is before Jordan" (1 Kgs 17:3). Elijah understood that he was to head eastward until he reached the Jordan River, then live on the bank of a brook that ran into it. *Cherith* means "a cut" or gorge, which would be a good place to hide. Elijah

> went and did according unto the word of the Lord: for he went and dwelt by the brook Cherith, that is before Jordan. And the ravens brought him bread and flesh in the morning, and bread and flesh in the evening; and he drank of the brook (17:5–6).

Elijah was a faithful man, saying what God told him to say, going where God told him to go, and doing what God told him to do without complaint or question. He was an obedient believer. By telling him where to hide and how to survive, God comforted him. Elijah had nothing to fear.

The drought eventually posed a problem.

> And it came to pass after a while, that the brook dried up, because there had been no rain in the land. And the word of the Lord came unto him, saying, Arise, get thee to Zarephath, which belongeth to Zidon, and dwell there: behold, I have commanded a widow woman there to sustain thee (1 Kgs 17: 7–9).

When the brook dried up, God commanded Elijah to go north of Israel to Zarephath (or Sarepta), on the Mediterranean coast between Sidon and Tyre.

> So he arose and went to Zarephath. And when he came to the gate of the city, behold, the widow woman was there gathering of sticks: and he called to her, and said, Fetch me, I pray thee, a little water in a vessel, that I may drink (17:10).

As she left to get water for him, he added, "Bring me, I pray thee, a morsel of bread in thine hand" (17:11). She halted. Apparently she was willing to bring water but not bread.

God had commanded the widow to sustain Elijah, but she balked at Elijah's command to bring bread to him. She sinned, but not deliberately. Out of fear that she and her son might starve, she explained "As the Lord thy God liveth, I have not a cake, but an handful of meal in a barrel, and a little oil in a cruse" (17:12). Elijah told her, "Fear not; go and do as thou hast said: but make me thereof a little cake first" (17:13). She was not to fear starvation because God promised to provide her with food: "For thus saith the Lord God of Israel, The barrel of meal shall not waste, neither shall the cruse of oil fail, until the day that the Lord sendeth rain upon the earth" (17:14). Even though she and her son were starving, the woman did not fear because of the promise of the Lord, "and she went and did according to the saying of Elijah: and she, and he, and her house, did eat many days" (17:15). As an act of repentance and of faith, the widow fed Elijah her last meal. She believed Elijah—that neither the barrel nor the pitcher would empty—and her belief was rewarded with miraculous sustenance for herself and her household for a year. Her rescue from sin (fear) was followed by a rescue from starvation.

Her faith was challenged again when her son unexpectedly died. She could not understand why, and she began to suspect his death had somehow been caused by her visitor whose promise was fulfilled by God. She became frightened of both his purpose and his power: "What have I to do with thee, O thou man of God? art thou come unto me to call my sin to remembrance, and to slay my son?" (17:18). She questioned why God had sent Elijah to her, and she asked if he came to punish her for her past sins. In short, she did not know why he was there, and she began to suspect that he had not come to help her. She was in danger of fear undermining her faith again, and because she did not know that she was tempted by sin, she was helpless to escape the danger.

Elijah called on God to resurrect her son in order to rescue the widow from sin. The command for her part in the rescue was simple: Elijah told her to "Give me thy son. And he took him out of her bosom, and carried him up into a loft, where he abode, and laid him upon his own bed" (17:19). The widow obeyed Elijah, giving up the body of her son to his care. His prayer was an intercession as much for her as it was for her son:

> And he cried unto the Lord, and said, O Lord my God, hast thou also brought evil upon the widow with whom I sojourn, by slaying her son? And he stretched himself upon the child three times, and cried unto the Lord, and said, O Lord my God, I pray thee, let this child's soul come into him again. And the Lord heard the voice of Elijah; and the soul of the child came into him again, and he revived (1 Kgs 17:20–22).

God created a means by which Elijah could work a miracle to strengthen the belief of the widow. God was spiritually rescuing the widow from sin by physically resurrecting her son. The boy's resurrection reassured her that there was no reason to fear punishment from God or Elijah, but there was every reason to believe that Elijah was sent by God to strengthen her both spiritually and physically. "And the woman said to Elijah, Now by this I know that thou art a man of God, and that the word of the Lord in thy mouth is truth" (1 Kgs 17:24). Her confession of belief in God ("the word of the Lord in thy mouth is truth") included belief in Elijah as a prophet. If anything, her belief in Elijah confirmed her belief in God. She became an obedient believer again, rescued twice from the unintentional sin of fearfulness, and rescued twice physically—once from death by starvation and once from the death of her son. Both physical rescues were miracles.

An even greater spiritual rescue was in the future for the nation of Israel. Unknown to Elijah, Ahab had been diligently searching for him, and Jezebel had been murdering the prophets of God. God commanded Elijah to leave Zarephath and appear before Ahab to prophesy the end of the drought (1 Kgs 18:1). Ahab's principal servant, Obadiah, encountered Elijah while Elijah was on his way to see Ahab. *Obadiah* means "servant of God" in Hebrew. The writer tells us that "Obadiah feared the Lord greatly" (18:3) so much so that when he met Elijah, he fell on his face and asked, "Art thou that my lord Elijah?" (18:7). Elijah's fame had spread. Obadiah reported that "As the Lord thy God liveth, there is no nation or kingdom, whither my lord hath not sent to seek thee: and when they said, He is not there; he took an oath of the kingdom and nation, that they found thee not" (18:10). Elijah was not the only prophet that Ahab and Jezebel could not find. Obadiah told Elijah about "what I did when Jezebel slew the prophets of the Lord, how I hid an hundred men of the Lord's prophets by fifty in a cave, and fed them with bread and water" (18:13). Obadiah begged Elijah to stay where he was, so that he could report to Ahab his whereabouts, and Ahab could meet him without danger of Obadiah being accused of a false report or worse, conspiring with Elijah.

Ahab came to Elijah to confront him with a question: "Art thou he that troubleth Israel?" (1 Kgs 18:17). From Ahab's point of view, Elijah was the cause of the drought, which had lasted over three years. Elijah responded, "I have not troubled Israel; but thou, and thy father's house, in that ye have forsaken the commandments of the Lord, and thou hast followed Baalim" (18:18). Elijah's counter-accusation seemed to trouble Ahab. He did not imprison Elijah or hand him over to Jezebel. Instead, he helped Elijah set up a contest at Mount Carmel between Baal on the one hand and God on the other hand to help the people determine whom they should follow.

Ahab revealed himself to be a believer in Baal, but not a strong believer. He had been persuaded by his wife Jezebel to have "forsaken the commandments of God" (1 Kgs 18:18) and become an unbeliever. Compared to the other kings of Israel,

> there was none like unto Ahab, which did sell himself to work wickedness in the sight of the Lord, whom Jezebel his wife stirred up. And his did very abominably in following idols, according to all things as did the Amorites, whom the Lord cast out before the children of Israel (1 Kgs 21:25–26).

Ahab rejected God and his word as a result of the influence of Jezebel, and he became an idolater, worshipping them in the way of the Amorites.

"All Israel" (1 Kgs 18:19) gathered to watch. "And Elijah came unto all the people, and said, How long halt ye between two opinions? if the Lord be God, follow him: but if Baal, then follow him. And the people answered him not a word" (18:21). The Israelite people were uncertain. The practice of worshipping God was being suppressed, and the practice of idolatry seemed to flourish with many places of pagan worship and hundreds of pagan priests. Some Israelites of the time were unbelievers because they had followed their king and queen, rejecting God and his word. Others may have been polytheists, worshiping God and Baal. In either case, they were unbelievers. They were in spiritual danger and helpless to escape their unbelief without turning to God and repenting.

The contest provided evidence that God was the only God of Israel. When the prophets of Baal came to sacrifice a bull to their false god, their prayers to accept the sacrifice came to nothing, and Elijah mocked them. When Elijah sacrificed a bull to God, he prayed "let it be known this day that thou art God in Israel, and that I am thy servant, and that I have done all these things at thy word" (1 Kgs 18:36). Further, he prayed that "this people may know that thou art the Lord God, and that thou hast turned their heart back again" (18:37). Elijah prayed for both a miracle to confirm that God was the only God and for the people to repent of their sins of unbelief and idolatry. In short, Elijah prayed for their spiritual rescue.

God answered Elijah's prayer with the miracle for which he asked. "The fire of the Lord fell, and consumed the burnt sacrifice, and the wood, and the stones, and the dust, and licked up the water that was in the trench" (18:38). This miracle inspired fear of God in the people: "And when all the people saw it, they fell on their faces: and they said, The Lord, he is *the* God; the Lord, he is *the* God" (18:39, emphasis added). They humbled themselves [by falling flat on their faces], prayed to God, and sought a relationship with God as their God. They confessed their belief in God as the only God of Israel and repented of their beliefs in other gods. Elijah commanded the people to "Take the prophets of Baal; let not one of them escape. And they took them: and Elijah brought them down to the brook Kishon, and slew them there" (18:40). The people did exactly what they were commanded to do ("take the prophets," "let not one escape") in order to complete their spiritual rescue. The deaths of the false prophets were legal executions of those who had spoken "in the name of other gods" (Deut 18:20).

As God told him to do, Elijah prophesied to Ahab the end of the drought: "Get thee up, eat and drink; for there is a sound of abundance of rain" (1 Kgs 18:41). Ahab did exactly as he was told,

Elijah repeatedly prayed for rain, "and there was a great rain" (18:45). The rain signaled a miraculous physical rescue of "all Israel" from a deep drought. With rain, crops could grow and the threat of starvation ended, fulfilling the promise by God to Solomon many years earlier:

> If I shut up heaven that there be no rain, . . . if my people, which are called by my name, shall humble themselves, and pray, and seek my face, and turn from their wicked ways; then I will hear from heaven, and will forgive their sin, and will heal their land (2 Chron 7:13–14).

God kept His promise to "heal their land" with rain.

The Israelites were rescued from their unbelief by repenting of their sin, and once they demonstrated their obedient belief, they were miraculously rescued from death. "If ye walk in my statutes, and keep my commandments, and do them; Then I will give you rain in due season, and the land shall yield her increase, and the trees of the field shall yield their fruit" (Lev 26:3–4). When the drought ended, God kept His promise of life to a justified people. "For I will have respect unto you, and make you fruitful, and multiply you, and establish my covenant with you" (Lev 26:9). Under these conditions (i.e. faithfulness to His commands and statutes), God promised a renewal of the blessing to Adam (Gen 1:28).

By the direction of God and supernatural strength (1 Kgs 18:46), Elijah ran ahead of Ahab to Jezreel, a fortress where Ahab held court and where Jezebel undoubtably was waiting for news. Ahab reported what had happened, including how Elijah had slain all the prophets of Baal. Jezebel's response put Elijah, who was probably in the city to support the king's obedient belief, in immediate physical danger. She "sent a messenger unto Elijah saying, So let the gods do to me, and more also, if I make not thy life as the life of one of them by to morrow about this time" (1 Kgs 19:2). Jezebel knew exactly where Elijah was, and she vowed to kill him within a day as punishment for demonstrating the power of God and killing the prophets of Baal.

Without waiting for instructions from God, Elijah fled. He "was afraid and got up and ran for his life" (1 Kgs 19:3 NASB) to Beer-sheba, which was a town in the far south of Judah, on the edge of the Negev Desert, about 100 miles away. This time, God had not provided a hiding place for him. He was on his own, driven by a fear of death and doubting God's power to protect him. He left his helper in Beer-sheba, and he withdrew a day's journey into the desert (another 20 miles to the south). Now alone and without help, food or even water, Elijah was on a suicide mission. He prayed to God, "and he requested for himself that he might die; and said, It is enough; now, O Lord, take away my life; for I am not better than my fathers" (1 Kgs 19:4). His conclusion, "I am not better than my fathers," probably meant that he considered himself a dead man walking, not unlike the Israelites of the exodus.

Jezebel had used a threat, backed by a history of killing prophets, to terrorize Elijah. He feared Jezebel to the point where he believed more in her ability to kill him than in God's power to save him. Much later, Jesus warned His disciples about this sin: "Fear not them which kill the body, but are not able to kill the soul: but rather fear him which is able to destroy both soul and body in hell" (Matt 10:28). Jesus warned them to fear neither man nor woman who threatened to kill them more than they feared God, who condemns sinners to hell. To have such fear is a sin because it denies the power of God to rescue the faithful from sin and death (or "them which kill the body").

In the case of Elijah, we are looking at the consequences of Elijah's failure to believe that God would use that power to protect him, a faithful person, even though God had used it twice in the last three years to protect him from evil. God commanded Elijah to:

- Flee Ahab and Jezebel's palace and "hide thyself by the brook Cherith"(1 Kgs 17:3) where he was sustained by ravens; and when the brook dried up,
- "Arise, get thee to Zarephath, which belongeth to Zidon, and dwell there" (17:9) to be sustained by a widow.

In both of these instances, he was spiritually rescued from sin and physically rescued from death at the same time. During this period, Ahab was searching for him. Hidden where God had commanded that he go, Elijah was saved from whatever evil Ahab planned to do to him (spiritual rescue), and at the same time, he was saved from starvation (physical rescue). This time, his fear of Jezebel overwhelmed his faith in God's power to rescue him from sin and death. He was terrified and alone in the desert, wishing to die. He was in spiritual danger and helpless to escape on his own.

There is no record in the Bible of any pursuit of Elijah out of Jezreel, let alone out of Israel, then finally a day's journey into the southern desert. Possibly no one was sent after Elijah to kill him or bring him back to Jezreel. No one needed to be sent. Terror alone seems to have driven Elijah into the desert to die. Had Elijah died in the desert as he wished, the outcome would have been far better for Jezebel than anything she could have imagined. Without lifting a finger let alone being implicated in his murder, she could have led Elijah to kill himself. He would have broken a commandment—thou shalt not kill—intentionally, and he would have died in sin. With God's help, Elijah had just spiritually and physically rescued Israel from non-belief. His suicide would have been an enormous come-back victory for Jezebel.

Mercifully, God sent an angel to Elijah to rescue him from dying. "And as he lay and slept under a juniper tree, behold, then an angel touched him, and said unto him, Arise and eat" (1 Kgs 19:5). The angel from God provided Elijah with not just food and water but the commandments to "arise and eat," demonstrating God's power to preserve his physical life, and assessing his willingness to obey and live. The angel supplied Elijah with encouragement. He was not alone. Through an angel, God was attentive to his physical and psychological needs, even when Elijah was a straying believer. God was gracious.

During a second visit, the angel gave him more food and water "because the journey is too great for thee" (19:7). What journey? Elijah apparently decided to seek safety in the Mount of God (19:8), another name for Mount Sinai or Mount Horeb. Once there, he hid in a cave. He had survived his suicide attempt, but he had not escaped his extreme fear of Jezebel, nor his doubt of God's rescue of obedient believers from sin and death. Undoubtedly, he thought that a cave in God's mountain was a safe place to hide because no one—except God—knew where he was.

God asked, "What doest thou here, Elijah?" (19:9). Elijah answered,

> I have been very jealous for the Lord God of hosts: for the children of Israel have forsaken thy covenant, thrown down thine altars, and slain thy prophets with the sword; and I, even I only, am left; and they seek my life, to take it away (19:10).

God's question could have led Elijah to reflect on his own fear, but still terrorized by Jezebel's threat, Elijah offered more excuses for his presence at Mount Sinai. They reveal that Jezebel had been able to seduce his mind with false beliefs, because his excuses reflected her point of view.

Her point of view was believable, but it was a lie. The truth was 1) Elijah was no longer zealous but discouraged and in hiding; 2) the people of Israel (including Ahab) had just become obedient believers, legally executing over 400 priests of Baal; 3) at least 100 prophets of God had survived Jezebel's persecution; and 4) Jezebel had vowed to kill him within a day, but he did not know if anyone actually sought after him. Her point of view was seductive, but Elijah knew the truth from his own experience and the testimony of Obadiah. His extreme fear had led him to believe what Jezebel wanted him to believe. She knew how to insinuate a spirit of fear into the mind of her adversary to intimidate him. She was an expert seductress and terrorist.

In answer to Elijah, God called him to the entrance of the cave and revealed to him a violent wind, an earthquake, and a fire, but God was not in the wind, nor in the earthquake, nor in the fire. Instead, God spoke in "a still small voice" (1 Kgs 19:12), giving Elijah an opportunity to listen carefully to the same question that He asked before, "What doest thou here, Elijah?" (19:13). God gave him a second chance to identify his sin, which was fear that caused him to doubt God's ability to preserve the faithful from sin and death. Elijah repeated his lament, demonstrating that his mind had not changed. He was still consumed by his fear of Jezebel.

God knew that Elijah's work as a prophet had come to a full stop, but it was not done. Israel would soon turn back to idolatry, and Ahab and Jezebel would continue to rule wickedly. God gave Elijah a set of commands that were sequenced like a procedure to remove the influence of Ahab and Jezebel from Israel:

> And the Lord said unto him, Go, return on thy way to the wilderness of Damascus: and when thou comest, anoint Hazael to be king over Syria [Damascus-Aram]: And Jehu the son of Nimshi shalt thou anoint to be king over Israel: and Elisha the son of Shaphat of Abelmeholah shalt thou anoint to be prophet in thy room. And it shall come to pass, that him that escapeth the sword of Hazael shall Jehu slay: and him that escapeth from the sword of Jehu shall Elisha slay. Yet I have left me seven thousand in Israel, all the knees which have not bowed unto Baal, and every mouth which hath not kissed him. (1 Kgs 19:15–18)

These three commands ("anoint," "anoint," "anoint") followed by three promises drew Elijah out of his hiding place and put in motion a plan to end Ahab and Jezebel's reign of terror and Israelite idolatry. They are extraordinary commands and promises if only for their impact on the history of Israel.

God's commands were fulfilled by a combination of Elijah, Elisha, and one of the "sons of the prophets" or the disciples of Elijah. The destruction of Ahab's family (including Jezebel) could end Elijah's fear of her, but it would not have led to his repentance. Just the opposite. The removal of the temptress would have left him in sin, like a thorn in his flesh only the exposed end of which would be removed. These commands were not for Elijah's spiritual rescue, but for the spiritual and physical rescue of the 7,000 "which have not bowed unto Baal," all presumably obedient believers. Their spiritual rescue would occur at the same time as their physical rescue through the deaths of their spiritual oppressors. Elijah was not an obedient believer, but a straying believer. God's rescue of him from fear would have to play out through another series of events.

God called Elijah to meet with Ahab to prophesy the punishment of Ahab and the destruction of Ahab's family, including Jezebel. Through Elijah, God said, "I will bring evil upon thee, and will take away thy posterity, and will cut off from Ahab him that pisseth against the wall, and him that is shut up and left in Israel" (1 Kgs 21:21). When Ahab heard that he was cursed, and that all of his male children would be killed, he humbled himself: "he rent his clothes, and put sackcloth upon his flesh, and fasted, and lay in sackcloth, and went softly" (21:27). Ahab mourned. God said to Elijah, "Seest thou how Ahab humbleth himself before me? because he humbleth himself before me, I will not bring the evil in his days: but in his son's days will I bring the evil upon his house"(1 Kgs 21:29). In response to Ahab's humbling himself, God also repented and delayed the promised executions (through Hazael and Jehu). God allowed Ahab to die in battle with the Assyrians before Hazael was anointed king of Damascus-Aram (also called Syria; see both maps). God's delay of His destruction of Ahab's family until after Ahab died may be why God used the next generation of prophets after Elijah (Elisha and the "sons of the prophets") to accomplish most of the tasks initially given to Elijah.

Ahab's son Ahaziah ruled after him as king of Israel, with Jezebel as the queen mother. (It is likely that Ahaziah was unmarried because he had no children.) "He did evil in the sight of the Lord, and walked in the way of his father, and *in the way of his mother*" (1 Kgs 22:52, emphasis added). Albert Barnes commented, "in this phrase, which does not occur anywhere else, we see the strong feeling of the writer as to the influence of Jezebel."[2] Ahaziah was an unbeliever. As queen mother, Jezebel apparently helped her son rule by counseling him, just as she had counseled her husband. Under the rule of Ahaziah (and his mother), Israel worshipped Baal again, and that angered God.

An accidental fall in the palace at Jezreel caused Ahaziah to be seriously injured. He sent messengers to a pagan oracle to learn whether or not he would live. The angel of the Lord, whom we have met before, commanded Elijah to "Arise, go up to meet the messengers of the king of Samaria, and say unto them, Is it not because there is not a God in Israel, that ye go to inquire of Baalzebub the god of Ekron?" (2 Kgs 1:3). This rhetorical question was a rebuke to Ahaziah, who intended to consult an oracle of the god of the Philistines in the city of Ekron (Amos 1:8) rather than a prophet of God. Further, the angel of the Lord gave Elijah a message for Ahaziah that promised his death: "Now therefore thus saith the Lord, Thou shalt not come down from that bed on which thou art gone up, but shalt surely die" (2 Kgs 1:4). Ahaziah would die in his bed before he could leave it because he had chosen to send his prayer request to a false god instead of to the Lord. His unbelief rather than his injuries would kill him. Undoubtedly, this message angered Ahaziah and his mother.

After hearing from his messengers, Ahaziah did not humble himself and repent as his father Ahab had done. He sent a captain and 50 men to Elijah, presumably to bring him to the palace to kill him, either because of his message, his mother's old promise, or both. The captain found Elijah sitting at the top of a hill. He said, "Thou man of God, the king hath said, Come down" (1:9). In response to this disrespectful order, Elijah called down fire that "consumed him and his fifty" (1:10). The king sent another captain and his 50 men. He gave a similar command, "Come down quickly" (1:11). Elijah again called down fire, which consumed them. Ahaziah sent a third captain and his 50, but this captain approached Elijah with humility. He went up, "fell on his knees before Elijah, and besought him, and said unto him, O man of God, I pray thee, let my life, and the life of these fifty thy servants, be precious in thy sight" (1:13). The captain transformed the summons of the king from a command to an humble request. "And the angel of the Lord said unto Elijah, Go down with him: be not afraid of him. And he arose, and went down with him unto the king" (1:15). Elijah came down the mountain to confront the king with God's message.

Such a simple act on Elijah's part revealed much. By obeying the commands of the angel, Elijah confronted the source of his terror, which was the influence of the queen mother. She was an unbeliever and out to destroy worship of God, as apparently was her son. The two commands given to Elijah ("go down with him" and "be not afraid of him") were commands to be obeyed as part of his rescue from fear. By going down from the mountain with the captain, Elijah repented of the fear that had earlier caused him to flee Jezreel for Mount Sinai. His righteousness was restored after he obeyed these two commands. As an obedient believer, he confronted the unbelieving king.

Elijah repeated for the king the same message that God gave to him earlier:

> Thus saith the Lord, Forasmuch as thou hast sent messengers to inquire of Baalzebub the god of Ekron, is it not because there is no God in Israel to inquire of his word? therefore thou shalt not come down off that bed on which thou art gone up, but shalt

surely die. So he died according to the word of the Lord which Elijah had spoken (2 Kgs 1:16–17).

The time between the two identical messages had given Ahaziah an opportunity to humble himself and turn to God, but he did not humble himself, pray, or seek God, let alone repent. God promised the unbelieving Ahaziah that he would die not from his injuries but from his wickedness, and he did. The miracle was not in his death but in its timing. Through Ahaziah's sudden death in his bed, God rescued Elijah from what would have surely been an execution that day. His physical rescue followed his rescue from fear, another sign of God's protection of the faithful from sin and death.

Today, fear of a terrorizing person can lead anyone to sin by fearing the terrorist more than fearing God. A terrorizing person will change the tone of a relationship, a home, a workplace, a city, a nation or even a church in a heartbeat to try to rule by intimidation, seduction, or both. As we have learned, however, obedient believers were rescued from sin and death, if they remained faithful. The spiritual rescue of Elijah was necessary because at one point, he did *not* believe that God would save him. God, of course, did save him spiritually and physically, repeatedly and dramatically.

How should faithful Christians deal with a "Jezebel?" One example occurred at a church in Asia called Thyatira. "I have a few things against thee," said Jesus, "because thou sufferest that woman Jezebel, which calleth herself a prophetess, to teach and to seduce my servants to commit fornication, and to eat things sacrificed unto idols" (Rev 2:20). Apparently, elders and members had allowed someone to teach false doctrine because the teacher (man or woman) had intimidated and seduced them physically, spiritually or both. Jesus saw a parallel with Jezebel and Elijah. Whatever danger this false teacher posed to them through physical seduction, seductive thoughts, a whisper campaign or an outright threat, the faithful should have confronted "Jezebel" with the truth: False teaching was going on, and it must stop. Instead, like Elijah, they avoided a confrontation, apparently hoping that the false teacher would go away without their opposition.

Christ would assume the burden of their sin, so that they would become aware of what they had done, repent of their fear, and always be ready to confront teachers of false doctrine. He said, "And I gave her space to repent of her fornication; and she repented not" (2:21). Christ provided a space of time for "Jezebel" to repent of teaching false doctrine and related sins, but He knew that there would be no repentance from this unbeliever. "Behold, I will cast her into a bed, and them that commit adultery with her into great tribulation, except they repent of their deeds" (2:22). Christ promised to punish the false teacher and anyone who had been seduced to believe in false doctrine with "great tribulation" until they repented. Beyond that, He promised to destroy anyone else who, having been taught false doctrine, intimidated the faithful in order to continue to teach lies: "And I will kill her children with death; and all the churches shall know that I am he which searcheth the reins and hearts" (2:23). Jesus referred to the unbelieving Ahaziah, Jezebel's son, who continued in the evil ways of his mother, and whom God killed because of his intentional sin. Rarely do we see Jesus promise to kill someone, but after the sinners had been warned, the punishment of death fit the crime of intentional sin.

Christians always have the word of God to help rescue them from fear of religious terrorists, whether in church or in the world, but Christians also must be ready to do their part by standing up to the bullies and refuting their doctrine. "Stand fast in one spirit, with one mind striving together for the faith of the gospel; And in nothing terrified by your adversaries: which is to them an evident token of perdition, but to you of salvation, and that of God" (Phil 1:27–28). God rescues from evil the faithful defenders of His gospel. As for Christ, "he hath said, I will never leave thee, nor forsake thee. So that we may boldly say, The Lord is my helper, and I will not fear what man shall do unto me" (Heb 13:5–6). Christ deflects the fear that bullies hope to inspire in the faithful by giving Christians a reason to be bold—Christ will never leave nor forsake them.

STUDY QUESTIONS

1. Think of a time when fear of someone—what they might think, say or do—tempted you to sin out of fear of them. How did you handle the situation? Could you have handled it better? If so, what would you have said or done?
2. Elijah was known for his zeal. Christians are also to be known for their zeal (Titus 2:14). How does Christian zeal differ from the zeal shown by Elijah? (Hint: Luke 9:51–56)
3. Jesus taught that repentance is demonstrated through actions (Matt 21:28–31). What actions did Elijah take to demonstrate repentance?
4. "The angel of the Lord" appears numerous times in the Old Testament. What is his role in the rescue of Elijah? How does his role here resemble his role in other spiritual rescues?
5. How many times was Elijah rescued from sin and death through God's protection of the faithful? Make a list yourself, then compare it with others' lists.

11

RESCUE FROM WILLFUL SIN

Jonah

> Now the Lord had prepared a great fish to swallow up Jonah. And Jonah was in the belly of the fish three days and three nights. Then Jonah prayed unto the Lord his God out of the fish's belly, And said, I cried by reason of mine affliction unto the Lord, and he heard me; out of the belly of hell cried I, and thou heardest my voice (Jonah 1:17–2:2).

If you were to ask someone whom did God rescue in the Old Testament, the answer probably would include Jonah. People remember his rescue because of its miraculous, physical nature: Jonah was swallowed by a great fish and stayed in its belly three days and three nights before being "vomited out" alive on dry land (Jonah 2:10). What did this miracle signal? If we dig into the story of "Jonah and the great fish," we begin to understand it as a story of spiritual rescue, in which God rescued Jonah from intentional sin.

We met the distinction between intentional and unintentional sin earlier, first in Chapter 3, where Elihu threatened Job with the charge of "rebellion" over and above self-righteousness. Job had not been rebellious, but even the thought of this "added" sin frightened him. Elihu told Job that "rebellion" or intentional sin was punishable "to the utmost" or by death. In Chapter 5 we learned that the intentional sins of the Sodomites and Lot's wife were punished by death, whereas Lot was spared by God's mercy because his sins were unintentional. We focused on the intentional sins of the Israelites during the exodus (Chapter 7), and we learned how through self-deception they undid their spiritual rescue from idolatry, resulting in the death of all but two of those who were adults when they left Egypt. In Chapter 9, we learned that David deserved death for his transgressions, but because he humbled himself, prayed for mercy and deliverance, and sought a closer relationship with God, God allowed him to repent and spared his life. With only this one exception, intentional sin led to certain death. In the book of Jonah we have an answer to the question, "Who can be spiritually rescued?"

Jonah was a prophet of God who lived in the Northern Kingdom (or Israel) during the reign of Jeraboam II, the 13th king of Israel (c. 786–746 BC). Jeraboam's reign was a prosperous time, but beginning in 740 BC, Israel's distant neighbor to the northwest, Assyria, conquered Aram-Damascus (Syria), attacked Israel, and began deporting Israelites to Assyria. In 722 BC, the Assyrians captured Samaria, Israel's capital city, and deported much of the rest of the population. At the time of Jonah, the Assyrians had not yet attacked Israel. Nineveh was the capital of Assyria, where Jonah was told to go preach: "Now the word of the Lord came unto Jonah the son of Amittai, saying, Arise, go to Nineveh, that great city, and cry against it; for their wickedness is come up before me" (Jonah 1:1–2). The Ninevites were unbelievers—they deliberately sinned. Their wickedness was the result of their conscious violation of natural law, just like the wickedness of the Sodomites (see Chapter 5). The prophet Nahum would curse their lifestyle: "Woe to the bloody city! It is all full of lies and robbery; the prey departeth not"

(Nahum 3:1). It was a place of continuous victimization. God commanded Jonah to go to Nineveh to preach to the wicked Ninevites.

Nineveh was located on the eastern bank of the Tigris River near modern-day Mosul. During the 8th Century B.C., it was an "exceeding great city" (Jonah 3:3). At the time of the story, it was perhaps the largest city in the world both in terms of physical size and population, estimated to be 600,000.[1] Its location was over 500 miles from Jonah's home town, which was Gath-hepher (2 Kgs 14:25). By way of contrast, Gath-hepher was only a small village located an hour's walk from Nazareth, much later the boyhood home of Jesus. God's command to Jonah to go to Nineveh required a journey that would have lasted about a month.

When God commanded Jonah to go preach there, Jonah went in the opposite direction.

> But Jonah rose up to flee unto Tarshish from the presence of the Lord, and went down to Joppa; and he found a ship going to Tarshish: so he paid the fare thereof, and went down into it, to go with them unto Tarshish from the presence of the Lord (Jonah 1:3).

Jerusalem, the capital of the Southern Kingdom (Judah), was where the Temple of God was located. The Temple was where many Jews believed that God lived because it housed the Ark of the Covenant. When Jonah received the commandments from God to "Arise, go to Nineveh" and "cry against it," he apparently believed that God's commandments came from the Temple. As a consequence, Jonah sought to flee from "the presence of the Lord" by traveling as far as he could away from the Temple in Jerusalem. That is probably why he chose Tarshish as his destination. Although the location of Tarshish is not known, it is widely believed to have been somewhere along the western coasts of the "Great Sea" or the Mediterranean, over 1,000 miles from Jerusalem.

Jonah thought that he could escape from the authority of God by physically distancing himself from the Temple, but he had only put himself in spiritual danger by disobeying the commandments of God. Further, his plot to escape God's authority revealed that he was not only disobedient but rebellious. Later in the story, we discover that the cause of his disobedience was self-centeredness, but the deliberateness with which he disobeyed God (i.e., by finding a ship and paying for a voyage that would take him as far as possible from the Temple) took his sin to a new level, which was rebellion or intentional sin. If there ever were someone who became an unbeliever, it was Jonah.

The ship on which Jonah fled set sail from Joppa to Tarshish, "But the Lord sent out a great wind into the sea, and there was a mighty tempest in the sea, so that the ship was like to be broken" (Jonah 1:4). As the ship began to take on water, the sailors did whatever they could to lighten it so that it would not sink:

> Then the mariners were afraid, and cried every man unto his god, and cast forth wares that were in the ship into the sea, to lighten it of them. But Jonah was gone down into the sides of the ship; and he lay, and was fast asleep. So the shipmaster came to him, and said unto him, What meanest thou, O sleeper? arise, call upon thy God, if so be that God will think upon us, that we perish not. (Jonah 1:5–6)

The captain woke up Jonah not to get him to safety but to order him to pray to his God "if so be that God will think upon us, that we perish not." The captain was not aware of the spiritual danger Jonah was in, but he knew the physical danger that the ship was in. He understood that despite their best efforts, the crew was helpless to save the ship from sinking in the storm. He believed that only a divine rescue could save them. Similar to God, the captain commanded Jonah to "arise" or get up, which Jonah did, but Jonah disobeyed the captain and did not pray to God. He was willfully disobedient. Jonah became physically awake, but he was willfully in sin and spiritually "asleep" or unresponsive.

Instead of praying, Jonah waited while the sailors "cast lots, that we may know for whose cause this evil is upon us" (Jonah 1:7). Casting lots was a time-honored way to let their gods make a decision; among the Israelites, it was a way to determine God's will, particularly who in a group might be guilty of sin (Josh 7:14; 1 Sam 14:42). When the lot fell on Jonah, the sailors interrogated him about his occupation, country and beliefs. "And he said unto them, I am an Hebrew; and I fear the Lord, the God of heaven, which hath made the sea and the dry land" (1:9). Jonah professed his faith, but this profession was not an admission of sin. The sailors challenged him, however, when he told them why he was on the ship: "Then were the men exceedingly afraid, and said unto him, Why hast thou done this? For the men knew that he fled from the presence of the Lord, because he had told them" (1:10). Jonah did not answer their question.

Jonah was now awake, both physically and spiritually. He had acknowledged his belief in God, and he had begun to feel ashamed of and guilty for his decision to flee "from the presence of the Lord." God had not let him get away. Jonah now believed that the storm was punishment for his misdeed, and if he did nothing, they were all going to die for it. He knew that death was the punishment for deliberate sin, but he also knew that the captain and his crew did not need to die because they had not sinned deliberately.

The sailors continued to talk about what they should do to be saved from the storm.

> Then said they unto him, What shall we do unto thee, that the sea may be calm unto us? for the sea wrought, and was tempestuous. And he said unto them, Take me up, and cast me forth into the sea; so shall the sea be calm unto you: for I know that for my sake this great tempest is upon you (Jonah 1:11–12).

Jonah found the obvious solution to their dilemma: Throwing him into the sea would appease God, calm the storm, and save the lives of the sailors. Jonah volunteered to appease God.

The sailors began to believe in God. They had initially shouted for help from other gods because they were in mortal danger and helpless, but the storm raged on. Their gods were unable to rescue them, so they abandoned them and turned to Jehovah God to rescue them:

> Nevertheless, the men rowed hard to bring it to the land; but they could not: for the sea wrought, and was tempestuous against them. Wherefore they cried unto the Lord, and said, We beseech thee, O Lord, we beseech thee, let us not perish for this man's life, and lay not upon us innocent blood: for thou, O Lord, hast done as it pleased thee. So they took up Jonah, and cast him forth into the sea: and the sea ceased from her raging (Jonah 1:13–15).

The sailors, who were Gentiles and non-believers, converted from whatever beliefs they had to believe in God. After they became believers, they accepted Jonah as a prophet, and following the instructions from God through him, they threw him overboard. Adam Clarke commented that the purpose of their prayer was "to call God to witness that it was with the utmost reluctance, and only in obedience to his command" that they threw Jonah into the sea.[2] They established their obedience to God when they followed the command exactly as it was given, doing their part in their spiritual rescue, and the effect of their repentance was to cleanse the ship from sin. Jonah had not yet repented.

The sea miraculously calmed, which both rewarded their obedience and rescued them from drowning. "Then the men feared the Lord exceedingly, and offered a sacrifice unto the Lord, and made vows" (1:16), thanking God and making promises to please Him. We recognize this pattern from other cases. It was a "double rescue," reflecting God's rescue of the faithful from sin and death.

RESCUE FROM WILLFUL SIN

"The Lord had prepared a great fish to swallow up Jonah" (1:17), which it did. Jonah turned to God for help:

> I cried by reason of mine affliction unto the Lord, and he heard me; out of the belly of hell cried I, and thou heardest my voice. For thou hadst cast me into the deep, in the midst of the seas; and the floods compassed me about: all thy billows and thy waves passed over me. Then I said, I am cast out of thy sight; yet I will look again toward thy holy temple (Jonah 2:2–4).

God gave Jonah his wish to go as far as possible from the presence of the Lord, which was not some distant city but "the belly of hell." The Hebrew for "hell" here is *Sheol,* which is more accurately translated as "Hades" (NASB). Hades was not considered a place of permanent punishment, which was properly known as *Gehenna* (a transliteration of *Hinnom,* the Hebrew name of a valley to the south of Jerusalem, used to burn refuse). In Hades, Jonah's soul was as far as it could be *spiritually* from God without being in a place of permanent punishment. Before Jonah was swallowed by the great fish, he had declared to the sailors his belief in God, but he had not repented of his sin.

Did Jonah really die? Some people say that Jonah had a near-death experience, but they forget that Jesus referred to His own death and resurrection as "the sign" or miracle of Jonah:

> An evil and adulterous generation seeketh after a sign; and there shall no sign be given to it, but the sign of the prophet Jonas: For as Jonas was three days and three nights in the whale's belly; so shall the Son of man be three days and three nights in the heart of the earth (Matt 12:39–40).

It is impossible to deny the death and resurrection of Jonah without denying the death and resurrection of Christ. Both died, and both were miraculously resurrected to physical (not just spiritual) life. The principal difference was that Jesus died on the cross for the sins of mankind, while Jonah died in the belly of a fish as punishment for his willful sin.

Jonah prayed to God from Hades because of his physical affliction. He hoped that even though he was in that dark place, God would hear his plea for help, and He did (Jonah 2:2). Jonah described his condition with images from drowning as he looked at waves from below, then he said, "I am cast out of thy sight; yet I will look again toward thy holy temple" (2:4). In his prayer, Jonah humbled himself and turned to God for help. After his body sank to the sea floor in the fish's belly, Jonah prayed a second time. "I remembered the Lord: and my prayer came in unto thee, into thine holy temple. They that observe lying vanities forsake their own mercy" (2:7–8). Being raised as a Hebrew, Jonah knew specifically what to do to repent: Admit that he had sinned; describe his sin, and express remorse.

If we look at Jonah's second prayer carefully, we find these elements of repentance. Jonah had believed that he could escape the commands of God by putting distance between himself and the Temple in Jerusalem, a belief which he described as a "lying vanity," or a self-deception. He could not escape the authority of God no matter where he went. He expressed remorse because his sin led him to "forsake his own mercy," or give up the opportunity to be corrected by God. Instead, he was punished with condemnation (to Hades) and death. To atone for his sin, he continued with the promise "I will sacrifice unto thee with the voice of thanksgiving; I will pay that that I have vowed. Salvation is of the Lord" (2:9). At that point, God spoke to the fish, which vomited Jonah on dry ground, alive and an obedient believer. Jonah's spiritual rescue was shortly followed by his physical rescue from the dead, which suggests that he was rescued from the dead *because* he became an obedient believer. Had he not humbled himself, prayed, sought God and repented of his sin, we should not expect him to have been physically rescued from death.

In their sequence, the two prayers of Jonah bear a strong resemblance to David's four penitent psalms (see Chapter 9). The parallels between Jonah's prayers and David's psalms do not suggest a common source as much as they imply a common process for dealing with deliberate sin. The process of returning to God begins with humility, recognizing personal helplessness apart from God (Jonah 2:1–4a). Help is then sought from God first through His listening to prayer, then His answering it (2: 4b–6). Finally, a closer relationship to God is sought (2:7), which requires repentance (2:8–9). The process of returning to God is necessary for the unbeliever to return to a right relationship with God, but it is not sufficient. The unbeliever has only become a straying believer. The willfulness of intentional sin is gone, but sin remains in some particular form of disobedience. That is why Jonah prayed twice. His second prayer represented his repentance.

At God's second call to Jonah to go preach at Nineveh, we see a closer relationship between God and Jonah than at first.

> And the word of the Lord came unto Jonah the second time, saying, Arise, go unto Nineveh, that great city, and preach unto it the preaching that I bid thee. So Jonah arose, and went unto Nineveh, according to the word of the Lord (Jonah 3:1–3).

This time, Jonah did exactly what God commanded him to do: 1) he rose up; 2) he went to Nineveh; and 3) he preached what the Lord commanded: "Yet forty days, and Nineveh shall be overthrown" (3:4). He preached a sermon that promised both a future event and when it would occur, which are defining features of a prophecy.

Jonah hoped that the Ninevites would be rebellious, and that God would destroy Nineveh after the forty days' grace period, but the people of Nineveh "repented at the preaching of Jonas" (Matt 12:41):

> So the people of Nineveh believed God, and proclaimed a fast, and put on sackcloth, from the greatest of them even to the least of them. For word came unto the king of Nineveh, and he arose from his throne, and he laid his robe from him, and covered him with sackcloth, and sat in ashes (Jonah 3:5–6).

Beginning with belief in the word of God, the king humbled himself, and he commanded that the people and even the animals "not feed, nor drink water" (3:7) and cover themselves with sackcloth to show remorse for their sins. Further, their king commanded them to "cry mightily unto God" (3:8a) or pray for reconciliation with him. Finally, he commanded, "turn every one from his evil way, and from the violence that is in their hands" (3:8b), or in a word, repent. By having his people obey his commands, the king hoped to avoid the promised destruction. Events in Nineveh generally fit in Table 3.

Why did the king and his people humble themselves so quickly and completely? One suggestion is found in the New Testament when Jesus said, "For as Jonas was a sign unto the Ninevites, so shall also the Son of man be to this generation" (Luke 11:30). For Jonah to have been recognized by both the king of Nineveh and his people as a "sign" or miracle, they must have known about his resurrection from the dead. The Ninevites believed that Jonah was a man who had returned from the dead with a prophecy of death and destruction aimed at them. He was highly believable because he was a living miracle sent to warn them.[3]

The Ninevites did their part in their rescue by turning to God and turning away from their sin. "And God saw their works, that they turned from their evil way; and God repented of the evil, that he had said that he would do unto them; and he did it not" (3:10). Through Jonah's preaching, God rescued the Ninevites from their deliberate sins. For a time, they became obedient believers. Their spiritual rescue was shortly followed by their physical rescue, as

God "repented of the evil" that destruction would have done to them. The spiritual rescue of the Ninevites (from unbelief) shortly before their physical rescue (from destruction) can be explained as another double rescue. The Ninevites' obedience to the righteous commands of their king, led God to rescue them from sin and death.

Jonah did not understand God's mercy towards the repentant Ninevites. God's mercy "displeased Jonah exceedingly, and he was very angry" (Jonah 4:1). His prayer to God explained why:

> I pray thee, O Lord, was not this my saying, when I was yet in my country? Therefore I fled before unto Tarshish: for I knew that thou art a gracious God, and merciful, slow to anger, and of great kindness, and repentest thee of the evil (4:2).

Jonah used some of the same words to describe God as God used to describe Himself (Exod 34:6–7). If we take Jonah at his word, the original reason that he had fled from "the presence of the Lord" was his belief that in the end, God would be merciful to the Ninevites and not destroy them with their city, when Jonah wanted them destroyed.

Why did Jonah want Nineveh destroyed? One reason could have been that Nineveh's destruction on the given day would confirm Jonah's prophecy: "Yet forty days, and Nineveh shall be overthrown." Had the "overthrow" occurred as he said it would, Jonah's identity as a prophet would have been confirmed along with his prophecy. If it did not occur, Jonah might be accused of being a false prophet.

> When a prophet speaketh in the name of the Lord, if the thing follow not, nor come to pass, that is the thing which the Lord hath not spoken, but the prophet hath spoken it presumptuously: thou shalt not be afraid of him (Deut 18:22).

Jonah would increase his reputation as a prophet if Nineveh were destroyed, but his reputation would decrease if Nineveh were saved. This reason for wanting the destruction of Nineveh is consistent with Jonah's self-centeredness. His primary concern was the effect of events on himself, not on carrying out the will of God.

A second reason that Jonah wanted Nineveh destroyed could have been that Jonah had no love for the Assyrians. They were not descended from Abraham, let alone Jacob (Hebrews), and more importantly, they were a growing threat to Israel. Within 50 years, Israel would be destroyed by the Assyrians. The ten Israelite tribes of the Northern Kingdom would be so completely deported and dispersed by the Assyrians that they would become known as the "Ten Lost Tribes of Israel." What God told Jonah to preach ("Yet forty days, and Nineveh shall be overthrown") raised Jonah's hopes that Nineveh—a threat to Israel—would be destroyed before the Assyrians could harm Israel. Jonah became angry when his hope of their destruction was crushed by God's mercy. Jonah's desire for safety for his country would be natural, but again, it would also be centered on self rather than on God, who takes "no pleasure in the death of the wicked; but that the wicked turn from his way and live" (Ezek 33:11). Safety lay not in eliminating the threat of Assyria but in the Israelites' faithfulness to God. "He will keep the feet of his saints, and the wicked shall be silent in darkness; for by strength shall no man prevail" (1 Sam 2:9).

A third reason that Jonah wanted the Ninevites destroyed could have been that he did not want Israel to include an overwhelming number of proselytes, known as "strangers." It was one thing for Israel to accept a boat's crew of "strangers" into their nation, but entirely another thing to accept 600,000 Ninevites. Although individuals such as Rahab could assimilate into Israelite culture rather easily, how could a huge number of proselytes from the middle of another nation (Assyria) with another language (Aramaic) be accepted without changing the Israelite culture to accommodate them? By persuading the Ninevites to turn to be obedient believers,

Jonah may have thought that he had created a huge problem for the Israelites. If this problem was the reason Jonah wanted the Ninevites destroyed, he again revealed that he was self-centered. Israel was to be a nation of God's people, not just Hebrews. Eventually, God's solution to this problem would be a spiritual kingdom rather than a physical kingdom. God "hath delivered us from the power of darkness, and hath translated us into the kingdom of his dear Son" (Col 1:13).

Whatever angered Jonah in the salvation of Nineveh also discouraged him. "Therefore now, O Lord, take, I beseech thee, my life from me; for it is better for me to die than to live" (Jonah 4:3). To teach Jonah about His mercy, God prepared an object lesson. Jonah built a booth on the eastern side of the city, hoping to watch Nineveh's destruction after 40 days. God grew a gourd plant beside it "to deliver him from his grief" (4:6), and Jonah was thankful for its shade. The next day, the plant withered; "and the sun beat upon the head of Jonah, that he fainted, and wished in himself to die" (4:8). God tried to teach Jonah that when God was compassionate towards him, Jonas was happy; when not, Jonah wanted to die. Jonah was all about Jonah. Why should God not then be compassionate towards the Ninevites, spare them, and make them happy, especially when there were "sixscore thousand" (120,000) young children there, and many cattle? The Ninevites were not Hebrew, but they obeyed God and kept his commandments, if only for a short while. The book ends, without an answer from Jonah.

What we see in the book of Jonah are three cases of "double rescue," that is, indications of God's rescue of the faithful from sin and death. What was new was the newly faithful were all Gentiles. The mariners on the ship to Tarshish came from diverse religious backgrounds because they initially "cried every man unto his god" for a rescue from the storm. The Ninevites were of Assyrian stock, only distantly related to the Hebrews. In short, the book of Jonah is about unlikely candidates for spiritual rescue (including Jonah), and how they came to be obedient believers.

One lesson to be learned by Christians is from our observation of Jonah himself. We each have a dynamic role to fill as a citizen in the kingdom of God, and that role is not entirely of our own choosing. We sometimes hear a child say, I am going to be _____ some day. Whatever we want to be is constrained by our God-given talents, and by what others will allow us to do. Jonah wanted to be a prophet, but he found himself in the role of an evangelist. The discovery of how we can best serve God should not cause discouragement but encouragement: There is a way for everyone to use their talents in God's kingdom, and the role may change as circumstances change. "Trust in the Lord with all thine heart; and lean not unto thine own understanding" (Prov 3:5). Failures can be more instructive than successes —just ask the young person who receives only A's in school. The marks may be rewarding, but instructive? Hardly. The young person in school needs discriminating feedback in order to learn about strengths and weaknesses. In religion as in education, we sometimes have to adjust our expectations to what we discover about ourselves through feedback. If Jonah had accepted the outcome God gave him at Nineveh, would he not have been happier in his service to God?

A second lesson to be learned has as much to do with the rescue of the mariners and the Ninevites as it has to do with Jonah. At the beginning of the chapter, the question was asked, "Who can be spiritually rescued?" The answer is anyone. A person does not need to be a Hebrew or a believer in God to be spiritually rescued. The person might even have rejected the truth of God's word, or violated natural law routinely. Even before Christ's ministry on earth, God used people like Jonah to rescue non-believers and even unbelievers from sin. Jonah himself was spiritually in unbelief, but by turning to God, then turning away from his sin, he was restored as an obedient believer and resurrected to life. One would think that through his miraculous rescue, he would have been compassionate towards the Assyrians, but he was not. He failed to understand that God's mercy was not tied to a nation. The lesson to be learned by the Christian is that personal background does not matter when it comes to a spiritual rescue. Anyone can be spiritually rescued.

A third lesson that Christians can take away from the book of Jonah is that nothing is too difficult for God. He can take someone who has rejected God and who is dying at the edge of hell, and restore them into an obedient believer, if they turn to Him and away from their sin. He can also assimilate obedient believers into Christ's church by the thousands. On the day of Pentecost, He brought 3,000 people from different nations and languages into the church at one time, then dispersed them to their native countries to spread the good news in their native languages. Although not everyone is Christian, Christians are everywhere, leading others to Christ. Jesus said "All power is given unto me in heaven and in earth" (Matt 28:18). No problem is too difficult for God and Jesus Christ to solve, particularly the problem of admitting new members to Christ's church.

STUDY QUESTIONS

1. Most of the book of Jonah is about willful sin, as is Hebrews 10. In your own words, what does willful sin include? How would you recognize it today?
2. Finding your way out of deliberate sin is like finding your way out of a forest. How do you determine North? Spiritually, what does that represent? Once you determine North, how do you find the direction you need to go?
3. Review the reasons that Jonah lacked compassion for the Ninevites. What was their root cause? How did God try to teach Jonah to change?
4. What causes people to lack compassion for sinners

today? How can you demonstrate compassion for an unintentional sinner? What about a willful sinner?

5. People sometimes want to be Christians who have family or personal circumstances that would make it painful for them to do so. How should you respond to people with such problems?

12
CONCLUSIONS

This book began with an idea of what a spiritual rescue is, and the purpose of the book was to test the idea using case studies from the Old Testament. A spiritual rescue was defined as "an escape from a spiritually dangerous situation that requires spiritual help." Added to this definition was a description of the process of a spiritual rescue. The process began with belief in God. In the middle of the process were commands for the rescue, and at the end of the process was obedience to these commands. The definition of a spiritual rescue set the boundaries of cases so that we had units for analysis, and the description of the process gave us criteria for analysis. Consequently, we could focus on whether or not belief, commands, and obedience were present in each case and how they might relate to each other.

In the end, the model proved a good framework for defining a spiritual rescue, especially with its classification of belief into four categories: unbelief, non-belief, straying belief, and obedient belief. The process of belief-commands-obedience described many spiritual rescues accurately, and the relative weight of each of the three components added insight to the interpretation of each story. Spiritual rescues of unbelievers, non-believers, and even some straying believers who were in doubt required that belief be established or strengthened before commands could be obeyed. To strengthen belief in Him and His word, God supplied promises, sometimes supported by miracles. Promises were most easily identified through grammar, as described in Chapter 1. Sometimes (as in the cases of Abraham, Sarah and Hagar) promises strengthened belief sufficiently to bring about obedience without much by way of command. The relative weight of the four components of the process changed from case to case, as we might expect in any set of rescues. In only one case was one of the components was entirely missing. David discovered how to turn to God for forgiveness, and as chief judge over Israel, he knew what repentance required. God rescued him from multiple sins and death, but David did not need to follow commands directed at him to do his part.

In addition to these findings, a broader model of the rescue process emerged that captured some unexpected but intriguing results. This model is based not on the experience of the rescued, but on a limited, third-person point of view, which is the point of view of much (but not all) of the narrative in the Bible. It is a view of a reporter of an incident rather than a participant in the incident. It is not an objective point of view, but it does capture the action in a wider scope than the direct experience of one or two people.

When we broaden the scope of a rescue to describe it from a limited, third-person point of view, we discover that a rescue is almost always preceded by a *search*. The search may be more or less systematic, but we often combine it with a rescue, as in "a search and rescue mission." From the perspective of the rescued person, the search may play only a small part in the mission, but from the perspective of the rescuer, it may make up almost all of the mission, and the rescue only a small part. We need to consider what a spiritual rescue looks like from the limited, third-person point of view if we want to include the entire process of "search and rescue."

REVISED MODEL OF THE PROCESS OF A SPIRITUAL RESCUE

The framework for analysis of a rescue led not only to many particular insights into events in the Bible, but as discussed, the application of the framework to events also led to insights about the model itself. The time has come to revise the model in light of what has been discovered. This reconsideration of results incorporates the original model into a broader view of the process. This broader concept of a spiritual rescue involves 1) an approach by God to mankind, 2) an opportunity for rescue from sin, and 3) a miraculous rescue from death. This revision of the process of a spiritual rescue included unexpected findings from case studies that the narrower model could not accommodate.

Approach of God to Mankind

Rather than begin with a component of a rescue, a broader approach to describe a spiritual rescue in the Old Testament would begin with God's approach to mankind. People may or may not have been in distress, and He may have approached people with a promise or a command or a miracle, but God always made the first move. If He was needed for a rescue, He was there, even before people called on him. The agency by which He chose to approach people was as variable as the need of the person or people whom he approached. He may have used his own words or reputation, or he may have sent a lawyer, one or more ordinary men, an angel, a woman, a prophet, an evangelist, or even a great fish. All served God as agents of God, but He approached people in need of a spiritual rescue before they approached Him. Today, most of us have God's word always near through the Bible, but the living God knows our needs even before we can express them (Matt 6:8), and He can use any agency that He wishes to do His will.

The state of belief in the people approached in the Old Testament did not seem to matter, although the message did. He approached unbelievers (those who rejected Him, His word or natural law) with a promise of destruction or a warning or a command to cease doing evil. This warning generally gave the unbeliever(s) a space of time in which to repent. He approached non-believers (who were non-committal or unaware of God) with an opportunity to repent of their non-belief as well as to repent of any sin that they had committed. He approached straying believers (who believed in Him but who sinned unintentionally) with an opportunity to become aware of and repent of their specific sin. Finally, he approached obedient believers with an opportunity to be rescued from the captivity of an evil society. He had a somewhat different approach to people in different states of belief so that they could draw closer to Him, if they believed His promises and followed His commands.

The God of the Old Testament was no different in this respect than the God of today, except that today He has chosen to communicate His will exclusively through the Bible, and He has chosen to receive prayers exclusively through Jesus Christ. These choices do not limit His choice of agents to do His will. He still can use anyone or anything to effect a spiritual rescue.

Opportunity for a Spiritual Rescue

In every case examined in the Old Testament of an individual or group who was in spiritual danger and helpless to escape it, God provided them with the opportunity of a spiritual rescue. He provided *the* way of escape; in other words, the means for escape was described. Over time, even the means for unbelievers to escape unbelief (or trespass) became described, first by David (in Psalm 32), then by God to David's son Solomon (in 1 Chronicles 7). To turn (or return) to God, they had to humble themselves, pray to God, and seek a closer relationship with Him. Once they turned to Him, they were straying believers who needed to repent of their sins by admitting they sinned, describing their sin, and feeling and showing remorse. Once the former unbeliever had done these things, he or she became an obedient believer, established or restored in a right relationship to God. That was the substance of their spiritual rescue.

For non-believers and straying believers (both unintentional sinners), God did not promise destruction and administer punishment, but He offered persuasion and instruction instead. Persuasion came in different forms, depending on the need of the sinner. He made promises or worked miracles to strengthen their belief in Him; He provided information to address their ignorance of His will; He asked rhetorical questions to provoke memory of what they already knew but had neglected or forgotten. He had angels encourage them and tell them not to be afraid. In short, He persuaded them and taught them in order to rescue them from the ignorance, neglect or accident of unintended sin.

There were differences between the spiritual rescues of non-believers and straying believers. The repentance of non-believers included a confession of belief in God as their only God. Following their praise for God and Him alone, the former non-believer confirmed their faith by an initial act that established their obedience. For straying believers, the first steps of repentance were somewhat different. Through their words or actions, they admitted to sinning, but they also turned from their sin in a way that identified which natural law or command was broken, e.g., Hagar returned to Sarah to submit herself to Sarah's natural authority; Jacob prepared a generous gift for his brother Esau, punishing himself for his covetousness. Like unbelievers, both non-believers and straying believers still needed to express remorse.

After repenting of their sin, former unintentional sinners were received as obedient believers—the righteous or faithful. Following the instructions for their rescue was sufficient evidence of their obedience to change the status of their belief in the eyes of God. That was the substance of their spiritual rescue.

Spiritual rescues could be refused or ignored. In only one case was the spiritual rescue refused (Israelites of the exodus), and their refusal of rescue from idolatry led to their death in sin. In another case (Lot), the instructions for his last of three rescues were ignored, leading not to death but to remaining in sin.

Another pattern that we see in spiritual rescues is the expansion of the people who could access a rescue. If the access began with Enoch, Enoch alone was rescued by being taken; if it began with Noah, Noah and his family were rescued. With Job, we see the first straying believer rescued. With Abraham and Sarah, we see the first straying couple rescued. With Hagar, we see the first Egyptian rescued from non-belief; with Rahab, the first family of Canaanites. With David, we see the first rescue of an unbeliever; with Elijah's story, the first foreign widow rescued from sin (widow of Zarephath), the first straying prophet (Elijah himself), and the first unbelieving nation (Israel at Mt. Carmel). With Jonah we see the first group of non-believers from diverse nations spiritually rescued, the first unbelieving prophet, and the first unbelieving city. As we progress along a timeline of the Old Testament, we see spiritual rescues of people with more and more diverse backgrounds, including diverse spiritual backgrounds. The expansion quickly overran the idea of a Hebrew nation descended from Jacob, or even a nation descended from Abraham. This expansion appears to have been part of God's plan.

With respect to the offer of a spiritual rescue, the God of the Old Testament is the same today, with significant changes in the nature of spiritual rescues due to the advent of Jesus Christ. These changes can be discovered using case studies of spiritual rescues in the New Testament. The analysis of spiritual rescues by category of believer (i.e., unbeliever, non-believer, straying believer, and obedient believer) offers a promising framework with which to approach the component of "belief" in spiritual rescues.

Miraculous Rescue from Death

CONCLUSIONS

In 13 out of 15 cases examined in the Old Testament, a physical rescue either accompanied or followed a spiritual rescue. Table 4 summarizes these findings.[1]

TABLE 4

Spiritual Rescues, Physical Rescues and Miracles

Name	Spiritually saved from	Physically saved from
Noah	Evil world	Drowning*
Job	Self-righteousness	Expectation of death*
Abraham	Doubt	"Body now dead"*
Sarah	Doubt	"Deadness" of womb*
Hagar (2)	Doubt	Death from dehydration*
Lot (3)	[Unintentional sins]	Destruction of Sodom*
Jacob	Covetousness	Being murdered*
Israelites in exodus	[Idolatry]	Egyptian genocide*
Rahab (2)	Sinful city	Destruction of Jericho*
Israelite spies	Mission failure	Capture and execution
David	Multiple sins	Death sentence*
Widow of Zarephath (2)	Fear of starvation	Death by starvation*
Israelites	Idolatry	Death by starvation*
Elijah	Fear of person	Execution*
Mariners	Belief in false gods	Death from drowning*
Jonah	Intentional sin	Permanent death*
Ninevites	Wickedness	Destruction of Nineveh*

*Asterisk represents involvement of a miracle in the rescue; parentheses represent multiple rescues. Brackets represent failed rescues.

The table shows that if people were in spiritual danger and helpless to escape on their own, God offered them a spiritual rescue. If they accepted the offer and followed the instructions for the rescue, they *all* (13/13) were not only spiritually rescued, but they were physically rescued from the prospect of death or from death itself. Further, in 12 out of 13 cases, the physical rescue occurred through a miracle. These findings are astonishing. They suggest something more was at work than a series of double rescues.

The finding that *all* of the successful spiritual rescues were either accompanied or followed by physical rescues suggests that the two types of rescue were related, but the relationship was often unclear. Two exceptionally clear rescues in this regard were the spiritual rescues of Abraham and Sarah. Paul's comments on Abraham's rescue, and the Hebrew writer's comments on Sarah's rescue clarified why their "dead" bodies were rejuvenated so that they could miraculously conceive a child. Their rescue from "death" was a reward for their righteousness, which was established through their strengthened faith. Their faith had to be strengthened (by promises) first, which explains why their spiritual rescue had to precede their physical rescue. These insights into the relationship between spiritual and physical rescues provide a point of departure for looking at the testimony of participants. How did they think the "double rescues" were related?

Testimony from individual cases supports the conclusion that rescues from death were rewards from God for faithfulness. Elihu said of God, "He looketh upon men, and if any say, I have sinned, and perverted that which was right, and it profited me not; He will deliver his soul from going into the pit, and his life shall see the light" (Job 33:27–28). Elihu was only a man, but he appears to have been well-versed in divine law. He is a credible witness. He described what caused a physical rescue by God, stated as a principle that applies to anyone ("if any . . . God will"). This principle is that *God will rescue anyone from condemnation for sin and from death, if that person repents of their sins*. In other words, repentance causes both spiritual and physical rescues. Repentance, of course, leads to righteousness.

Consistent with Elihu but providing an even more penetrating analysis are the words of David. In Psalm 18, he claimed that physical rescues from God were rewards for his righteousness:

> He delivered [rescued] me [physically], because he delighted in me. The Lord rewarded me according to my righteousness; according to the cleanness of my hands he hath recompensed me. For I have kept the ways of the Lord, and have not wickedly departed from my God. For all his judgments were before me, and I did not put away his statutes from me. I was also upright before him, and I kept myself from mine iniquity. Therefore hath the Lord recompensed me according to my righteousness, according to the cleanness of my hands in his eyesight. (Ps 18:19–24)

According to David, his physical rescues by God were rewards (or recompense) from God for his righteousness. David reached this conclusion on the basis of his own experiences. If we combine David's personal insight with Elihu's knowledge of divine law, we reach the generalization that spiritual rescues in the Old Testament resulted in righteousness, which was rewarded by God with a physical rescue. In cases in which spiritual and physical rescues occurred at the same time, the rescued person was already righteous. In cases in which the spiritual rescue preceded the physical rescue, righteousness needed to be established by obedience to the instructions for the spiritual rescue before God rewarded the righteous with a physical rescue.

If we see the testimonies of Elihu and David as complimentary to the cases of Abraham and Sarah, we see the large scheme of rescue: For a sinner who has turned to God, repentance of sin causes righteousness, and righteousness pleases God. A rescue from death is God's reward for righteousness. This pattern is not new. It existed in the days of Enoch: "By faith Enoch was translated that he should not see death; and was not found, because God had translated him: for before his translation he had this testimony, that he pleased God" (Heb 11:5). Enoch was righteous, and his righteousness pleased God. As a reward for his righteousness (or for pleasing Him), God rescued him from death by translating him to what we may presume to be Paradise.

Were all the righteous rewarded with a miraculous rescue from death? Evidently not, as shown in the story of Cain and Abel, the first two sons of Adam and Eve. "By faith Abel offered unto God a more excellent sacrifice than Cain, by which he obtained witness that he was righteous, God testifying of his gifts" (Heb 11:4). Abel was righteous, but he was not rewarded with a rescue from an untimely death. "And it came to pass, when they were in the field, that Cain rose up against Abel his brother, and slew him" (Gen 4:8). Despite his righteousness, Abel was not rescued from being murdered by his brother. God gave Cain an opportunity to confess his sin, but he did not. God called on Cain to reflect: "And he said, What hast thou done? the voice of thy brother's blood crieth unto me from the ground" (4:10). Clearly, Abel was dead, but justice had not been done. God punished Cain by a curse from the earth, "which hath opened her mouth to receive thy brother's blood from thy hand" (4:11), condemning Cain to be a vagabond, and marking him, but still no rescue for Abel's soul until Judgment Day (Heb 11:13–16; Rev 6:9–11). In the Old Testament, God did not promise even a temporary rescue from death for the righteous. However, the association between spiritual and physical rescues was very close as revealed by Table 4 and as described in the Appendix.

ETERNAL LIFE AS A REWARD

We can say with certainty that the reward for faithfulness in the Old Testament was incomplete when contrasted with the reward for faithfulness under the New Testament. The rescue from death in the Old Testament, which was a reward for righteousness, was in two senses, temporary. It was temporary because it was not a permanent rescue from death, and it was temporary because it lasted as a reward for righteousness only until the advent of Jesus Christ.

The reward for faithfulness in the Old Testament was only a shadow of the reward to come. The Hebrew writers explained that Christ prayed fervently to God for a rescue from death.

> Who in the days of his flesh, when he had offered up prayers and supplications with strong crying and tears unto him that was able to save him from death, and was heard in that he feared; Though he were a Son, yet learned he obedience by the things which he suffered; And being made perfect, he became the author of eternal salvation unto all them who obey him (Heb 5:7–9).

The writer of Hebrews captured the process through which Christ became the means for "all them who obey him" to receive the reward of eternal salvation. God rescued Christ from the grave to make him an "high priest after the order of Melchisedec" (5:10), once king of Jerusalem. Jesus gave eternal life as the reward for all who would be faithful to Him.

The book of Hebrews describes other advantages of the new reward for righteousness over the old reward, perhaps the greatest of which is the promise in life of this reward. The old reward (a temporary rescue from death) was never promised to the righteous (see the example of Abel). But the Hebrew writer explained that Christ is "the mediator of the new testament, that by means of death, for the redemption of the transgressions that were under the first testament, they which are called might receive the promise of eternal inheritance" (Heb 9:15). We know "the called" are "all them that obey him," not some other special group of people. For them, the new reward for faithfulness to Him is a *promised* reward, whereas the old reward, though almost always given by God, was never promised.

We are very familiar with this new promise, but perhaps now we might appreciate it more than ever before. The promissory is God, but the promise was communicated through Jesus to Nicodemus: "For God so loved the world, that he gave his only begotten Son, that whosoever believeth in him should not perish, but have everlasting life" (John 3:16). *Should* does not introduce doubt. *Should* is the conditional form of *shall,* which when used in the third-person, indicates a promise. Jesus was telling Nicodemus that God promises everlasting life to whomever is an obedient believer in Jesus Christ as the Son of God. The necessity of obedient belief made the promise conditional. The faithful will be rescued from sin and death permanently, by Jesus, on Judgment Day.

Jesus is now God's means of rescue: "For God sent not his Son into the world to condemn the world; but that the world through him might be saved" (3:17). To be rescued permanently from sin, a person needs to follow Jesus by obeying His commands. Towards the end of His ministry on earth, Jesus told Thomas, "I am the way, the truth, and the life: no man cometh unto the Father, but by me" (John 14:6). "The way" was the way to heaven, or what in the Old Testament was called the "path of life." Jesus walked a path similar to the path walked by the righteous in the Old Testament. "Think not that I am come to destroy the law, or the prophets: I am not come to destroy, but to fulfill" (Matt 5:17). What had begun as a path in the Old Testament was redone in the New Testament, making its travel easier—just as many roads today are paths redone—and its destination clearer.

With the exceptions of Enoch and Elijah, God reserved eternal life as a reward for righteousness until after Jesus was crucified, buried and resurrected.

> And as it is appointed unto men once to die, but after this the judgment: So Christ was once offered to bear the sins of many; and unto them that look for him shall he appear the second time without sin unto salvation (Heb 9:27–28).

Jesus ascended to heaven, and He will come a second time for the purpose of rescuing the faithful in Him from sin and death, permanently.

The gift of Jesus Christ to humankind does not diminish the value of these case studies to identify the nature of spiritual rescues and trace their development through the Old Testament. Beginning with Noah, if not Enoch, God not only provided *the* way for a righteous person to be rescued from sin and from death, but he provided *the* way for a sinner, no matter how deep or how often the sin, to become faithful. He provided the way of salvation, incomplete as it was. Finally, God opened up this "path of life" to people from all nations and in all numbers. Even though the destination of the path was not yet attainable, it was at least in view as a city prepared by God for the faithful (Heb 11:16).

APPENDIX

Miracles as Rewards for Righteousness

A review of the cases shows how miraculous physical rescues operated as rewards for righteousness in almost every case of spiritual rescue investigated. The exceptions were Rahab's first rescue (from non-belief) and the rescue of the pair of Israelite spies, neither of which appears miraculous. Why miracles were absent from these cases is an unanswered question.

In the case of Noah, the miracle was not the rain, nor the flood, but a wind which dried the waters: "And God remembered [the covenant with] Noah, and every living thing, and all the cattle that was with him in the ark: and God made a wind to pass over the earth, and the waters asswaged" (Gen 8:1). The miraculous wind that dried the land was God's reward for Noah's righteousness. The wind ended the risk of drowning (physical rescue). Recall that the covenant with Noah is not given to us, but from its context can be determined to be something as simple as 'If you will be faithful, I will rescue you from sin and death.' When God remembered the covenant, He rewarded Noah with a rescue from death because Noah had remained righteous (or faithful).

In the case of Job, the miracle was release from the physical captivity of Satan. Recall that this captivity had been so brutal that Job wished to die. "And the Lord turned the captivity of Job, when he prayed for his friends: also the Lord gave Job twice as much as he had before" (Job 42:10). After Job repented of his sin of self-righteousness, God rewarded the restored righteousness of Job with a miraculous physical rescue. A miraculous material reward ("the Lord gave Job twice as much as he had before") accompanied the miraculous restoration of the health of his body.

In the cases of Abraham and Sarah, the miracle was the rejuvenation of their frail (even "dead") bodies. Earlier, 99-year-old Abraham had doubted God and laughed at the promise of a child by 89-year-old Sarah, and Sarah had laughed at the same news. Both repented of their doubt by strengthening their faith on no other basis than God's promises. Abraham

> staggered not at the promise of God through unbelief; but was strong in faith, giving glory to God; And being fully persuaded that, what he had promised, he was able also to perform. And therefore it was imputed to him for righteousness (Rom 4:20–22).

"Through faith also Sara herself received strength to conceive seed, and was delivered of a child when she was past age, because she judged him faithful who had promised" (Heb 11:11). Rejuvenation of their "dead" bodies (physical rescue) was the miraculous effect of their righteousness after their doubt disappeared because of God's promises.

In the case of Hagar, there were two spiritual rescues, one as a pregnant, run-away, non-believing servant and the other as a divorced mother of a 13-year-old child, straying from belief. In the first rescue, an angel of the Lord persuaded her of God's existence. She called on the name of the Lord, and repented of her disdain for Sarah by accepting the commands to "return" and "submit." The reward for her righteousness was removal from a physical dilemma that threatened her life (physical rescue). She considered her encounter with God to be miraculous (Gen 16:13). Thirteen years later, God rescued Hagar again. Abraham divorced Hagar, and he sent her into the desert with her son. She doubted God's promises for Ishmael's future. Her righteousness was restored after she believed in God's promise for her son: "I will make him a great nation" (Gen 21:18). "And God opened her eyes, and she saw a well of water; and she went, and filled the bottle with water, and gave the lad drink" (21:19). God gave Hagar the miraculous vision of water as a reward for her righteousness. The water saved her life and the life of her son (physical rescues).

In the case of Lot, three spiritual rescues were involved, two successful and one unsuccessful. During the first rescue, Abraham rescued "righteous Lot" from being a captive of Chedorlaomer and three other Mesopotamian kings. The miracle was the defeat of so many enemies by so few of Abraham's men that God "hath delivered thine enemies into thy hand" (Gen 14:20). God freed Lot from captivity much like righteous Noah was delivered from the captivity of a sinful world. The spiritual and physical rescues coincided because of Lot's righteousness. In Lot's second rescue, angels pulled him into into his house to prevent him from sinning and being crushed by the angry mob in Sodom. The angels worked a miracle, rewarding his righteousness by rescuing him from death by blinding them so that Lot could escape (physical rescue). Lot did escape, but in his third rescue, he did not obey instructions for the rescue. He "lingered" and later he balked at God's commands. If he had followed these commands, he would have been removed from evil influences, but he strayed from belief during the rescue attempt. The angels removed him from physical danger of being destroyed by God, not to reward Lot, but to reward Abraham for his righteousness. "God remembered [the covenant with] Abraham, and sent Lot out of the midst of the overthrow, when he overthrew the cities in the which Lot dwelt" (Gen 19:29).

In the case of Jacob, the miracle accompanying his physical

rescue was his acceptance by Esau. Jacob prayed for physical rescue from his brother and prepared a gift as an atonement. He confessed his sin ("Heel Grabber" or "Supplanter") to an angel who wrestled with him. His righteousness was restored when God renamed him "Israel." As a reward for his righteousness, God rescued him from Esau (physical rescue). Jacob characterized the outcome of the meeting with Esau as a miracle: "I have seen thy face, as though I had seen the face of God, and thou wast pleased with me" (Gen 33:10). His righteousness restored, God's gift was the favor of his brother (physical rescue).

In the case of the exodus, God worked his miracles to remove the Israelites from Egypt. With only two exceptions, the adult Israelites of that generation were never faithful (Heb 3:10). The miracles worked by God were never rewards for their righteousness, but the means by which God kept His promise that "I will bring you up out of the affliction of Egypt" (Exod 3:17). "I wrought [miracles] *for my name's sake,* that it should not be polluted before the heathen, in whose sight I brought them out" (Ezek 20:14, emphasis added). The miracles preserved His reputation from being "polluted" or blemished. God's reputation for faithfulness would be preserved for the next generation so that they (without their unbelieving parents) could conquer Canaan more easily.

Rahab was rescued twice, once from non-belief and once as an obedient believer. In the first rescue, the spies in her house not only witnessed her confession of belief (a spiritual rescue), but they provided her with a means to escape the utter destruction of Jericho (physical rescue). Her first spiritual rescue (spiritual conversion) occurred before her first physical rescue (escaping the destruction of Jericho) because her righteousness had to become established before her physical rescue could occur. More plainly, she had to become a proselyte Jew before the spies could rescue her. That makes sense, but where is the miracle in it?

Her second spiritual rescue was her escape from an evil society. Because she was already righteous, this spiritual rescue occurred at the same time as her second physical rescue, which was her miraculous escape from the collapse of the wall on which she lived. God afforded this escape as a reward for her faithfulness or righteousness. "By faith the harlot Rahab perished not with them that believed not, when she had received the spies with peace" (Heb 11:31). Her miraculous escape from the collapse of the wall (physical rescue) was the reason (over and above the scarlet rope) that the returning spies found her and her family alive.

The Israelite spies were rescued spiritually and physically only once, and because they were already obedient believers, their spiritual and physical rescues occurred at the same time. Recall that they were under orders (commands) to complete a mission. The mission started to fail almost as soon as it began because the king of Jericho knew who they were, what their mission was, and where they were. Rahab helped them to complete their mission (spiritual rescue), and at the same time, she helped them to escape their pursuers (physical rescue) by sending them for three days to the mountain that looked over the city. What was missing from their "double rescue" was a miracle, unless it was Rahab's willingness to send the spies out on faith. She entrusted them not only with her life, but the lives of all of her Canaanite family. Whether that trust —that faith—rose to the level of a miracle is a matter of interpretation. It is also possible that God helped rescue the spies, who never sinned, but that He was not well pleased with them.

In the case of David, the miracle was escape from a death sentence. "The Lord hath chastened me sore: but he hath not given me over unto death" (Ps 118:18). David was "chastened" to teach him to be a better king. His righteousness was restored after he confessed his sin and atoned for it with "a broken and contrite heart" (Ps 51:17). His escape from a sentence of death (physical rescue) was his miraculous reward for finding *the* way for an unbeliever to become an obedient believer (righteous) again, by turning to God before repenting.

In the case of the Widow of Zarephath, she was rescued from

sin twice. In her first spiritual rescue, she repented of her fear of starvation (and breaking God's command to sustain Elijah) by making her last meal for Elijah on faith. This repentance restored her righteousness. As a reward, God commanded a miracle: "The barrel of meal shall not waste, neither shall the cruse of oil fail, until the day that the Lord sendeth rain upon the earth" (1 Kgs 17:14). The miracle of the meal and oil saved their lives (a physical rescue) as a reward for her faithfulness. When the widow's son died, she feared Elijah was the cause, but she repented of her fear after Elijah commanded her to give the boy's body to him. After her repentance, God rewarded her righteousness, this time with the miraculous resurrection of her son (physical rescue).

In the case of the Israelites at Mt. Carmel (including Ahab), the miracle was rain. Under the influence of Jezebel, the Israelites had begun to worship alien gods as their gods. When they witnessed God win a contest between Elijah and hundreds of false priests, the people turned to God and repented of their sin. They proclaimed God as *the* God of Israel, and after confirming their belief by capturing all the false prophets, their righteousness was restored. Their righteousness was rewarded with rain, which ended the drought that had caused a famine (a physical rescue).

In the case of Elijah himself, the miracle was the sudden death of Ahaziah for his unbelief rather than his injuries. After Elijah repented of his fear of Jezebel by coming down the mountain, his righteousness was restored, and as a reward for Elijah's righteousness, Ahazian was killed by God while he was in bed, preserving Elijah's life (a physical rescue). God had said to Elijah about Ahab, "in his son's days will I bring the evil upon his house" (1 Kgs 21:29), which included the death of his first-born son. What was evil for Ahaziah was a miracle for Elijah, who otherwise had almost certainly been killed by Ahaziah (a physical rescue).

In the case of mariners on the way to Tarshish, the miracle that rewarded righteousness was the calming of the sea. The mariners were non-believers who lost faith in their gods to calm the storm.

They prayed to Jehovah God as their God, and they obeyed Jonah's command to throw him overboard, confirming their belief. Their righteousness was rewarded with the miraculous calming of the storm, which saved their ship from being wrecked (physical rescue).

In the case of Jonah himself, the miracle was resurrection from the dead. After Jonah died in unbelief, he turned to God and repented from Hades of the "lying vanity" that had led him to forsake God's mercy. As a reward for his restored righteousness, God miraculously resurrected him from the dead (physical rescue). "And the Lord spake unto the fish, and it vomited out Jonah upon the dry land" (Jonah 2:10).

In the case of Nineveh, God's repentance was the miracle. The Ninevites were Assyrian unbelievers, with a lifestyle that routinely broke natural laws. After Jonah preached their destruction to them, they believed him, turned to God and repented of their "evil ways." As a newly righteous people, God rewarded their righteousness with His own repentance. He decided not to destroy Nineveh (physical rescue). "God repented of the evil, that he had said that he would do unto them; and he did it not" (Jonah 3:10).

With the regularity of a drumbeat, people who were rescued from sin in a way that resulted in their righteousness were rewarded by God with a miraculous rescue from death. We can say that the relationship between spiritual and physical rescues was close, but the example of Abel shows that the righteous did not always receive a miraculous rescue from death. Even a temporary rescue from death in the Old Testament was not a promise to the righteous. The promise to the righteous of a permanent rescue from death would have to await the death, burial and resurrection of Christ.

NOTES

1. WHAT IS A SPIRITUAL RESCUE?

1. Natural law: "A body of unchanging moral principles regarded as a basis for all human conduct" (*Oxford English Dictionary*), discussed in greater detail in Chapter 2.
2. Occasionally, rescue commands used verbs in the "jussive" mood, as in "Let him answer it" (Job 40:2), or in Jonah 3:7–8, but this verb form was less common.
3. John Wallis, *Grammatica Linguae Anglicanae* (Oxford: 1653), 94–95. See also R. W. Burchfield, *Fowler's Modern English Usage,* rev. ed. (Oxford: Oxford University Press, 2004), 706–707.
4. Popular translations that respect this nuance are the ASV, RSV, NKJV, TYN, and WYC. Most contemporary translations (including the NASB) do not preserve it.
5. Both Christians and Jews are forbidden to experiment with spiritual rescues (Matt 4:7; Deut 6:16).
6. Edward W. Fudge, *The Divine Rescue* (Abilene, TX: Leafwood, 2010).
7. John MacArthur, *Twelve Ordinary Men* (Nashville, TN: Nelson, 2002).
8. Mark Jones, *Criminals of the Bible* (Grand Haven, MI: FaithWalk, 2006).
9. Complementarity in "*Physics*: The concept that two contrasted theories, such as the wave and particle theories of light, may be able to explain a set of phenomena, although each separately only accounts for some aspects." (*Oxford English Dictionary*).

2. RESCUE FROM AN EVIL WORLD

1. Bruce K. Waltke, *Genesis: A Commentary*. (Grand Rapids, MI: Zondervan, 2001), 140.
2. T. W. Brents, *The Gospel Plan of Salvation* (Nashville, TN: Gospel Advocate, 1973).
3. Albert Barnes, *James, Peter, John and Jude* (NNT 10; Grand Rapids, MI: Baker, 1979), 243.

3. RESCUE FROM SELF-RIGHTEOUSNESS

1. Adam Clarke, *Adam Clarke's Commentary on the Bible* (6 vols.; New York: Abingdon, n.d.), 3:143. See also Christopher Ash, *Job: The Wisdom of the Cross* (Wheaton, IL: Crossway, 2014), 325–330.

4. RESCUE FROM DOUBT

1. Mike Willis, *The Book of Genesis 1, 1-25a* (Truth Commentaries; Athens, AL: Truth Publications, 2021), 550.
2. James B. Coffman, *Commentary on Genesis* (Abilene, TX: ACU Press, 1985), 219.

5. FAILED RESCUE FROM UNINTENTIONAL SIN

1. Several descriptions of the eastern border of Canaan exist, but this one is taken from Numbers 34:12 and is consistent with several recent maps of ancient lands.

6. RESCUE FROM COVETOUSNESS

1. William Grasham, *Genesis*, 2 vols., Truth for Today Commentary (Searcy, AR: Resource Publications, 2014), 2:245–246.

7. RESCUE FROM IDOLATRY REFUSED

1. Robert Jamieson, A. R. Fausset and David Brown, *Commentary Practical and Explanatory on the Whole Bible* (Grand Rapids, MI: Zondervan, 1961), 696.

8. RESCUE FROM A SINFUL PAST

1. John MacArthur, *Twelve Extraordinary Women* (Nashville, TN: Nelson, 2005), 67.
2. Barnes, *James, Peter, John and Jude*, 243.

9. RESCUE FROM MULTIPLE SINS

1. Franz Delitzsch, *Biblical Commentary on the Psalms 2, 36–83,* trans. F. Bolton, repr., (Grand Rapids, MI: Eerdmans, 1955), 20.
2. Delitzsch, *Biblical Commentary on the Psalms 2, 36–83*, 23.
3. The other general description of rescues by God is in Job 33:27–28.

10. RESCUE FROM FEAR

1. After the death of David's son Solomon (around 930 BC), Israel split into the Northern Kingdom (which kept the name Israel) and the Southern Kingdom (which adopted the name of its largest tribe, Judah). The capital of Israel was Samaria, and the capital of Judah was Jerusalem.
2. See Albert Barnes, *Samuel-Esther,* NOT 4, (Grand Rapids, MI: Baker Book House, 1979), 225.

11. RESCUE FROM WILLFUL SIN

1. James B. Coffman, *Commentary on the Minor Prophets* (Abilene, TX: ACU Press, 1981), 1:280, 341. Population estimates vary. The number 600,000 is extrapolated from the number of young children (120,000) being one fifth of the population. See Jonah 4:11.
2. Clarke, *Adam Clarke's Commentary on the Bible*, 4:701.
3. Messages from the dead have always been highly sought. Recall the rich man in Hades who asked Abraham to send Lazarus from Paradise to warn his brothers on earth of torment in Hades: "If one went unto them from the dead, they will repent" (Luke 16:30).

12. CONCLUSIONS

1. The table does not account for multiple rescues of the same person except in parentheses immediately after the name of the case.

BIBLIOGRAPHY

Ash, Christopher. *Job: The Wisdom of the Cross*. Wheaton, IL: Crossway, 2014.

Barnes, Albert. *James, Peter, John and Jude*. Notes on the New Testament 10. Grand Rapids, MI: Baker, 1979.

———. *Samuel-Esther*. Notes on the Old Testament 4. Grand Rapids, MI: Baker, 1979.

Brents, T. W. *The Gospel Plan of Salvation*. Nashville, TN: Gospel Advocate, 1973.

Burchfield, R. W. *Fowler's Modern English Usage*. Rev. ed. Oxford: Oxford University Press, 2004.

Clarke, Adam. *Adam Clarke's Commentary on the Bible*. 6 vols. New York: Abingdon, n.d.

Coffman, James B. *Commentary on Genesis*. Abilene, TX: ACU Press, 1985.

_____. *Commentary on the Minor Prophets*. 4 vols. Abilene, TX: ACU Press, 1981.

Delitzsch, Franz. *Biblical Commentary on the Psalms 2, 36–83*. Translated by F. Bolton. Reprint. Grand Rapids, MI: Eerdmans, 1955.

Fudge, Edward W. *The Divine Rescue*. Abilene, TX: Leafwood, 2010.

Grasham, William. *Genesis*. 2 vols. Truth for Today Commentary. Searcy, AR: Resource Publications, 2014.

Jamieson, Robert, A. R. Fausset, and David Brown. *Commentary Practical and Explanatory on the Whole Bible*. Grand Rapids, MI: Zondervan, 1961.

Jones, Mark. *Criminals of the Bible*. Grand Haven, MI: FaithWalk, 2006.

MacArthur, John. *Twelve Extraordinary Women*. Nashville, TN: Nelson, 2005.

_____. *Twelve Ordinary Men*. Nashville, TN: Nelson, 2002.

Oxford English Dictionary. 3rd ed. New York: Oxford University Press, 2010.

Wallis, John. *Grammatica Linguae Anglicanae*. Oxford: 1653.

Waltke, Bruce K. *Genesis: A Commentary*. Grand Rapids, MI: Zondervan, 2001.

Willis, Mike. *The Book of Genesis 1: 1-25c*. Truth Commentaries. Athens, AL: Truth Publications, 2021.

SCRIPTURE INDEX

Old Testament
Genesis
1:28	168	14:19–20	81
2:6	33	14:20	211
3:7	14	15:2	61
4:8	204	15:4	61
4:10	204	15:5	61
4:11	204	15:6	61
5:24	36	16:1	62
6:5	27	16:2	62
6:5–7	28	16:3	63
6:9	29, 36	16:4	63
6:11	29	16:5	64
6:13	28	16:6	64
6:14–16	30	16:7	64–65
6:17	31	16:8	65
6:18	30	16:9	65
6:18–19	31	16:10	65–66
6:22	34	16:11	66
6:22–7:1	32	16:12	66
7:5	34	16:13	66, 211
7:8–9	34	17:1–2	68
7:21	34	17:16	68
8:1	34, 209	17:17	59, 68
8:15–19	35	17:19	69
8:21	28	17:20	69, 73
9:11–13	31	17:21	69, 74
11:26	63	18:1–2	69
12:1	20	18:3	69
12:1–2	100	18:9	69
12:1–4	60–61	18:10	71
12:4	61	18:10–12	69–70
12:10–20	78	18:13–14	70
13:8	79	18:15	71
13:10	79–80	18:20–22	81
13:13	79	18:23	82
14:3	80	18:32	82
14:4	80	19:1	82–83
14:10	80	19:2	83
14:12	80	19:3	84
14:17	81	19:4	84
14:18	81	19:5	84
		19:6–7	84
		19:7	82

19:8	84
19:9	85
19:10	85
19:12–13	86
19:14	86
19:15	86
19:16	78, 87
19:17	87
19:18–19	88
19:20	88
19:21–22	88
19:24	89
19:26	89
19:29	91, 211
19:30	89
19:32	89
20:1–18	78
20:18	78
21:3	73
21:6	73
21:10	73
21:11	73
21:13	73
21:14	74
21:15–16	74
21:18	74, 211
21:19	75, 211
25:22–23	94
25:26	94
25:27	94
25:28	94
25:29–33	95
25:34	95
26:2–3	100
26:34	94
27:1–5	96
27:8–10	97
27:13	97
27:28–29	98
27:36	98
27:41	98
27:42	106
27:42–45	98
28:2	98
28:12–13	99
28:14	99
28:15	100, 103
28:16	100
28:17	100
28:20–21	108
28:20–22	101
30:43	102
31:3	101–102, 108
31:7	102
31:13	101
32:3–5	102
32:6	103
32:10–11	103
32:12	104
32:13	104
32:20	104
32:24–25	105
32:26–27	105
32:27–28	93
32:28	93, 105
32:30	105
32:32	106
33:10	212
33:10–11	106
39:1	67
49:8	139

Exodus

3:5	111
3:13	111
3:14	111
3:17	114, 212
4:3	112
4:4	112
4:5	112
4:6–7	112
4:9	113
4:29–30	113
4:30	114
4:31	113
6:23	138
12:48	132
15:22–24	67
20:2–5	118
20:13	145
20:14	144
20:15	144
20:17	96, 142
22:1	96, 151
32:1–6	120
32:9	124
33:3	124
34:6–7	189

Leviticus

18:3	126–127
18:6–18	127

18:20	127	2:8–9	129–130
18:21	127	2:9	135
18:22	127	2:10	130
18:23	127	2:11	130
18:24–25	127	2:12–13	131
18:25	127	2:14	132
18:29	127	2:15	130
19:18	145	2:15–16	133
20:10	96	2:18–20	134
20:13	84	2:21	135
26:3–4	168	2:22	135
26:9	168	2:24	135

Numbers

7:11–12	138	5:7	135
11:21	110	5:9	135
13:32	117	5:10	135
14:9	135	5:14	135
14:27	121	6:5	136
14:30	121	6:16–17	136
15:22–29	152	6:20	136
15:31	152	6:21–22	136
20:11–12	92	6:23	137, 140
21:6	120	6:25	125, 137–138
21:29	89	7:14	183
24:18	94	24:2	59
25:1–9	120		
34:12n	218		

1 Samuel

2:9	190
14:42	183
16:7	154

Deuteronomy

2:24	127	**2 Samuel**	
2:25	128	11–13	145
2:30	127	11:1	143
2:34	127	11:2	143
3:3	127	11:2–3	142
5:3	117	11:4	144
6:16n	217	11:11	144
7:2	136	11:15	144
18:20	167	12:1	149
18:22	189	12:1–4	151
19:15	130	12:5	151
21:17	95	12:6	151

Joshua

1:16	125	12:7	151–152
1:17	128	12:9	152
2:1	125, 128	12:9–10	152
2:2	128	12:11–12	152–153
2:3	128	12:13	146, 160
2:4	129	12:13–14	153
2:4–5	129	12:14	148
2:6	129	**1 Kings**	
2:7	129	11:5	89
		11:7	89

15:5	145–146	22:52	174
16:33	161	**2 Kings**	
17:1	162	1:3	174
17:3	162, 170	1:4	174
17:5–6	162	1:9	175
17:7–9	163	1:10	175
17:9	170	1:11	175
17:10	163	1:13	175
17:11	163	1:15	175
17:12	163	1:16–17	175–176
17:13	163	14:25	181
17:14	163, 214	**1 Chronicles**	
17:15	163	7	198
17:18	164	**2 Chronicles**	
17:19	164	7:13–14	168
17:20–22	164	7:14	159–160
17:24	165	**Job**	
18:1	165	1:1	43
18:3	165	1:3	44
18:7	165	1:7	44
18:10	162, 165	1:8	44
18:13	165	2:4–6	56
18:17	165–166	2:9	44
18:18	166	2:10	44
18:19	166	2:11	44
18:21	166	2:13	44
18:36	167	3:24	48
18:37	167	4:8	44
18:38	167	6:24	45, 50
18:39	167	7:13–15	47–48
18:40	167	10:2–3	45
18:41	167	16:8	48
18:45	167	19:20	48
18:46	168	30:17	48
19:2	168	32:1–2	43
19:3	168	32:2	45
19:3–4	161	33:6–7	47
19:4	169	33:9–11	47
19:5	170	33:13	47
19:7	171	33:15	47
19:8	171	33:19–22	48
19:9	171	33:27–28	48, 202
19:10	171	33:27–28n	219
19:12	172	33:31–33	50
19:13	172	34:2–5	50
19:15–18	172	34:5	51
21:21	173	34:10–15	51
21:25–26	166	34:16–20	51
21:27	173	34:21–22	51
21:29	173, 214	34:24–25	51

34:26–29	51	51:10–12	156
34:31–32	51	51:13	156
34:33	51	51:16–17	156
34:35–37	51	51:17	213
35:2	52	95	123
35:3	52	118:18	157, 213
36:24–25	52	**Proverbs**	
36:26–28	52	3:5	192
36:29	53	30:21–23	63
37:1	53	**Isaiah**	
37:2	53	11:1–2	154
37:5	53	59:1	40
38:1–3	53	**Ezekiel**	
38:4	54	16:49–50	82
40:2	54	20:1	113
40:2n	217	20:3	113
40:4	55	20:4	113
40:4–5	54	20:6–8	113–114
40:6–8	54	20:7	118
40:9	55	20:7–8	109
40:14	55	20:8	114
42:2–6	55	20:9–10	115
42:10	56, 210	20:11–13	116
Psalms		20:14	116, 212
6	25, 145–147	20:15–16	117
6:1–3	146	20:17	117
6:4–5	146–147	33:11	190
6:9	147	**Hosea**	
6:10	147	12:4	105
18	203	**Amos**	
18:19–24	203	1:8	174
32	25, 145–146, 156–158, 198	**Jonah**	
		1:1–2	180
32:5	157	1:2	19
32:6–7	157	1:3	181
32:8–9	157	1:4	182
37:25	124	1:5–6	182
38	25, 145–150, 153, 160	1:7	183
		1:9	183
38:1	147	1:10	183
38:2	147	1:11–12	183
38:3	147	1:13–15	184
38:4–5	147	1:16	184
38:11–12	147	1:17	185
38:13–14	148	1:17–2:2	179
38:17–18	149	2:1–4a	187
38:21–22	149	2:2	186
51	25, 145–146, 155–156, 158	2:2–4	185
		2:4	186
51:1–3	155	2:4b–6	187

2:7	187
2:7–8	186
2:8–9	187
2:9	186
2:10	179, 215
3:1–3	187
3:3	181
3:4	187
3:5–6	188
3:7	188
3:7–8n	217
3:8a	188
3:8b	188
3:10	188, 215
4:1	189
4:2	189
4:3	191
4:6	191
4:8	191
4:11n	219

Micah

6:8	36

Nahum

3:1	180–181

New Testament

Matthew

1:1	154
1:4	138
1:5	138, 140
4:1–11	42
4:7n	217
5:17	206
6:8	197
6:13	139
6:24	122
6:33	124
9:13	32
10:28	169
12:39–40	185
12:41	187
19:14	13
19:26	140, 159
21:28–31	178
24:35–39	38
28:18	193
28:19–20	139

Mark

10:47	154

Luke

4:24	162
9:23	107
9:51–56	178
11:30	188
12:47–48	89
16:30n	219
17:28–33	90

John

3:16	24, 206
3:17	206
14:6	206

Acts

7:24–25	111
8:3–4	159
9:1	159
9:6	159–160
13:22	154

Romans

1:27	84
2:14–15	16, 28
3:23	13
4:18–22	71
4:20–22	210
6:17–18	22
15:4	22

1 Corinthians

10:1–4	119
10:5	119
10:6	120
10:7	120
10:8	120
10:9	120
10:10	120
10:11	121
10:12	122
10:13	37
10:13–14	122
15:33–34	90
15:51–52	39
15:54–57	37

2 Corinthians

7:8	90

Ephesians

1:1	17

Philippians

1:27–28	177
2:12	42, 153
2:12–13	39
2:15–16	39

Colossians
1:13	191

2 Thessalonians
3:3–4	39

1 Timothy
1:15	159

2 Timothy
3:2–5	29

Titus
2:14	178

Hebrews
3:8–9	123
3:10	212
3:10–11	123
3:12	16, 123, 159
3:14	123
4:12	90
5:7–9	205
5:10	205
9:4	122
9:15	205
9:27–28	206
10	193
11:4	204
11:4–5	33
11:5	203–204
11:7	33
11:11	72, 210
11:13–16	204
11:16	207
11:21	107
11:24–25	111
11:27	111
11:30–31	137
11:31	213
13:2	83
13:5–6	178

James
1:14–15	143
2:19	101
5:11	43

1 Peter
3:19	33
3:19–20	32
3:20	33
4:8	77

2 Peter
2:3	39
2:5	29
2:6	89
2:7	82
2:7–9	79
2:8	82
2:9	39

1 John
1:8–9	121–122

Revelation
2:20	176
2:21	177
2:22	177
2:23	177
6:9–11	204

ABOUT THE AUTHOR

John F. Wakefield is a an elder of the Atlas Church of Christ near Greenhill, Alabama, where he teaches adult Bible classes and occasionally preaches. He received undergraduate degrees in English literature and French linguistics, and a Ph.D in education from the University of Illinois. He taught educational psychology for 37 years at the undergraduate and graduate levels before his retirement in 2014. Towards the end of his college teaching career, he published articles about the influence of Christianity on the early development of American public schools. This book represents a groundbreaking application of case study methods to the analysis of scripture. He lives with his wife Janelle in Florence, Alabama.

ALSO BY CYPRESS PUBLICATIONS

Always Near by Bill Bagents

Easing Life's Hurts (2nd ed.) by Bill Bagents and Jack Wilhelm

Equipping the Saints (2nd ed.) by Bill Bagents and Cory Collins

Revisiting Life's Oases by Bill Bagents

Welcoming God's Word by Bill Bagents

King of Glory by Travis Bookout

Jesus the Christ by Ed Gallagher

The Holy Spirit by Jack Wilhelm

Visions of Restoration by John Young

CPSIA information can be obtained
at www.ICGtesting.com
Printed in the USA
JSHW021410090521
14450JS00001B/2